# Living Hope

## Reading 1 Peter Today

Paul Barnett

AQUILA PRESS

Published December 2006



Aquila Press, P O Box A287, Sydney South, NSW 1235, Australia.
www.youthworks.net
www.publications.youthworks.net

National Library of Australia
ISBN 1 921137 63 0

Designed and typeset by Lankshear Design

In Memory of
Bruce Leslie Smith,
*didaskalos*

(1932-2001)

# Contents

# The First Letter of Peter

Please read this first

## A warm and personal letter

To understand individual parts of a book like 1 Peter it is important to have some idea about its overall 'big picture' message. A good practical first step, then, would be to read the letter from beginning to end without interruption. That won't take very long since there are only 105 verses all together.

Peter wrote this letter in Rome for congregations scattered throughout five Roman provinces in northern Anatolia.[1] The messenger who brought the letter most likely read it as if it was a sermon from Peter to them. A local scribe would then copy the letter for that church's ongoing use. The messenger would then move on to the next church and stay for several weeks while the same process was repeated. It would have been many months before he reported back to Peter in Rome about the state of the churches and how the letter was received.

Peter's stated purpose in writing comes at the end of the letter.

> I have written to you briefly,
> *appealing* to you and *witnessing*
> that this is the true grace of God.
> Stand firm in it (5:12[2]).

Peter's 'I...appeal' appears also in two other passages:

> I *appeal* to you...to abstain from the passions of the flesh
> that wage war against your souls (2:11).

> I *appeal* to the elders among you...Tend the flock... (5:1-2).

---

1. Anatolia was the name then given to Asia Minor, that part of modern Turkey between the Mediterranean and the Black Seas.
2. My translation (also in 2:11 and 5:1) renders the verb *parakalo* as 'I appeal...'

Along with Peter's personal 'appeal' we note that he addresses his readers directly throughout as 'you'. Only rarely does Peter include himself with them as 'we' or 'us' (for example, 1:3; 2:24). 'I appeal to you' gives the letter a warm-hearted and practical feel. The modern reader can readily sense that he/she is included in the 'you' whom Peter is addressing.

### The 'shape' of the letter

There are five parts in the letter:

| | |
|---|---|
| 1:1-2:10 | God's new people |
| 2:11-3:8 | God's people in the world |
| 3:9-4:6 | Who will harm you? |
| 4:7-5:11 | The end is near |
| 5:12-14 | Final greetings |

The letter is a broad-brush sketch of the Christian life from beginning to end. Peter begins by assuring them of their beginnings (as re-born ones) and concludes by appealing to them to 'stand firm' (because the end is near). Between their beginning and the end he appeals to them to *behave appropriately* and not to fear their enemies. This is the sequence their own lives will follow from start to finish as God's people in a world where they are regarded as non-citizens and aliens.

There is a kind of narrative quality about this little letter-sermon, in two senses. First, in 1:1-2:10 Peter tells their story as members of the re-born Israel as it has unfolded. Second, in 2:11-5:11 he 'appeals' to them to make their ongoing story what it *should* be, to the very end.

### Rome and the Anatolian provinces

Peter writes from 'Babylon' (5:13), almost certainly a coded reference to Rome. He had founded churches in Jerusalem and in the land of Israel and visited churches in Syria (Antioch) and Greece (Corinth). To our knowledge he did not write to any of these churches. Why, then, did he write to believers in Pontus, Galatia, Cappadocia, Asia and Bithynia?

The most likely answer is that Peter visited Anatolia and preached there during his travels from Antioch (*ca* AD 48) to Corinth (*ca* AD 53) (see Galatians 2:11-13 and 1 Corinthians 9:5). He certainly reveals some familiarity with the circumstances of the readers (for example 1:12; 2:11, 15; 3:16; 4:4, 12). It is also possible that some of his readers had contacted him afterwards.

Mark also may have brought the good news of salvation to these Anatolians. We know that Mark visited Colossae in Roman Asia (Colossians 4:10; cf. 2 Timothy 4:11). Furthermore, Mark (through Peter) sent his greetings to these readers (5:13), implying that they knew him. On the other hand, Peter must introduce Silvanus ('a faithful brother, as I regard him'), implying most of the readers did not know him (5:12).

Did Paul preach to Peter's readers? It's true that Paul preached extensively in (southern) Galatia and in Roman Asia. Yet to our knowledge he did not visit the more northerly provinces of Pontus, Cappadocia or Bithynia. As well, First Peter gives no hint that the readers faced the problem created by 'agitators' (as in Galatians) who attempted to overturn Paul's 'law free' Gospel. It appears that Christianity in Anatolia resulted from missionary work that was somehow in parallel with Paul's, but which was not his. These Anatolian congregations do not appear to have been targeted by the 'judaisers' from Palestine.

There is one other possible group who may have evangelised northern Anatolia. We know that Jews from Cappadocia, Pontus, Asia and Phrygia (in southern Galatia) were in Jerusalem for the Feast of Pentecost and heard Peter proclaim Jesus as the Christ and the arrival of the Day of Salvation in his death and resurrection (Acts 2:9-10). Quite possibly numbers of these were baptised and instructed under Peter, and then returned to their homelands where, in turn, they preached the gospel and established churches. Something like this would explain the link between Peter and the Anatolian Christians, especially if Peter visited these provinces between AD 48-53, which he had opportunity to do—as noted above.

According to this reconstruction the foundation members of the Anatolian churches would have been converted Jews. This might help explain the various 'Jewish' elements within the letter, which we will find as we go through the text. Gentiles would have heard the gospel so that by the time Peter wrote the letter many of his readers (if not most of them) were from a non-Jewish background (cf. 4:3-4).

## Reading and teaching this letter

Six principles have guided me in writing about First Peter. They are general principles that apply to other parts of the Bible as well.

First, it is helpful to consult a Bible dictionary to find out as much as possible about when and why the letter was written, and under which circumstances.

Second, we should recognise that any individual part of First Peter must be understood in relationship with the whole letter. This is not difficult to do since the letter is quite short.

Third, it is important to understand that the basic 'building blocks' of the letter are the paragraphs, not the individual verses. Most modern translations helpfully divide the text into paragraphs, often with sub-headings.

Since the paragraph is key we need to ask ourselves, 'Where does this paragraph fit into the flow of the letter overall?' What is the previous paragraph about, and the one following?

Re-setting the text line by line helps us identify its structure. This is helpful because most editions of the Bible don't do this to conserve valuable space on the printed page. For example the RSV for 1:3-5 runs like this:

> 3 Blessed be the God and Father of our Lord Jesus Christ!
> By his great mercy we have been born anew to a living hope
> through the resurrection of Jesus Christ from the dead, 4
> and to an inheritance which is imperishable, undefiled, and

unfading, kept in heaven for you, 5 who by God's power are guarded through faith...

How different it looks when we re-set the text:

3 Blessed be the God and Father of our Lord Jesus Christ!
By his great mercy we have been born anew to a living hope
through the resurrection of Jesus Christ from the dead,
4 and to an inheritance which is imperishable, undefiled, and unfading,
kept in heaven for you,
5 who by God's power are guarded through faith...

Re-setting the text like this helps us find the structure that Peter so carefully crafted so that we can get inside his line of thought. We are able to:

(a) identify one main idea at a time since each line usually expresses one main idea;
(b) see how each line relates to the previous line and the line following;
(c) notice how a statement of fact on one line is substantiated in the next (introduced by 'for' or 'because') and is often followed in the next by a statement of purpose (introduced by 'that' or 'in order that');
(d) pick up repeating words, contrasting words, similar sounding words ('imperishable, undefiled...unfading').

Fourth, we need to do some research about words and ideas in the paragraph that are not clear to us from the translation we are using. This means looking up a commentary or Bible Dictionary, or both.

After this we get down to really hard work, that is, to work out what Peter really wanted his original readers to think and to do. Here we must be very disciplined and prayerfully objective. Otherwise we will jump from the text too quickly to our own 'theological grid' (which we all have!). But no; we must think Peter's thoughts because God put those thoughts into Peter's mind, through the Holy Spirit.

Finally, we reflect on our passage in the light of the

teaching of the Bible, globally speaking. Amber lights should be flashing if we begin to think Peter is teaching something that is out of line with a biblical teaching elsewhere. For example, some have argued that 3:19 and 4:6 support the idea that the deceased are given a second chance to repent. That idea is contrary to the teaching of the Bible overall and, upon examination, is not what Peter is teaching anyway.

We engage in these tasks prayerfully seeking God's strength to understand his Word, for it is *his* Word. In that regard, we seek the assistance of the Spirit of God to work out how this scripture applies to us today. That is the final task and it is vital that we don't run ahead to this point before we have done the other hard work beforehand.

These take time and self-discipline but the rewards are great. We will be, in Paul's words, 'workmen who have no need to be ashamed', since we are 'rightly handling the word of truth' (2 Timothy 2:15).

# 1

# God's New People

## 1 Peter 1:1-2:10

Running beneath Peter's text is the 'story' of Israel, which he re-tells in terms of its fulfilment in Christ. Peter signals key moments in that story at various points: The 'exiles...chosen and destined by God' (1:1) remind us of God's *choice* of Abraham and his descendants 'exiled' in Canaan.[3] The phrase 'ransomed *out of'* (1:18) refers to the Israelites' escape from slavery in Egypt that God made possible by the blood of the Passover *'lamb'* (1:19). Peter alludes to the events at Mt Sinai in his reference to 'sprinkling of the blood' (of oxen) and the injunction 'be holy' (1:2, 15). Peter points to the entry into Canaan, and subsequent loss of the land, when he speaks of 'an 'inheritance', that is 'imperishable, undefiled and unfading' (1:4). In the land the people have a temple and a priesthood (2:5) and they are 'God's own people' his 'holy nation' (2:9).

In Christ God has now re-told this great story, but perfectly and finally, so as to supersede the earlier version. Peter's present readers are God's re-born Israel. Yet God is still the same: at heart he is rescuer of slaves whom he ransoms, gives a secure inheritance and from whom he expects holiness and praise.

Peter reminds these readers scattered across northern Anatolia, Gentiles in the main, that previously they were not the people of God (2:10); they were trapped in a web of passions and futility (1:14, 18). But 'now' through the Gospel-word centred on the sufferings of Christ and his

3. Genesis 23:4 Abraham: 'I am an alien and a stranger among you' (NIV).

resurrection from the dead, they have been re-born to know the God of Israel as Father. They have been given a 'living hope' of an imperishable inheritance (1:3-4). In a powerful appeal to the original exodus Peter reminds them of the cost of their redemption out of the former way of living, with a strong call to holiness of life expressed in reverent fear (1:14-20).

Just as Israel was a covenant people with reciprocal responsibilities to their divine rescuer, so now they are a covenant people with reciprocal responsibilities to their redeemer (1:22; 2:1). These responsibilities are 'shaped' by the life and teaching of Christ, his service of others and the example of his sufferings.

## THE OPENING (1:1-2)

Letter writing at that time followed fairly strict conventions. First the writer gave his name; mostly it was 'he' since few women could read or write. Then he stated his relationship with the readers (father, brother, friend, official position). Next came the name of the addressee with a prayer to the gods or a devout wish for the health and well-being of the recipients.

As we read Peter's opening sentences we can see that he is following the format for letter writing, but with two major differences. First, Peter has 'christianised' the formalities, and second, the letter is not written to an individual but to many people scattered over a vast area. Like the book of Revelation (which is also written in the form of a letter) Peter intended his letter to be taken from place to place by a messenger, where it would be copied for reading in each local church. It is a 'circular' letter.

1 *Peter, an apostle of Jesus Christ,*
*to the exiles of the dispersion in Pontus, Galatia, Cappadocia, Asia, and Bithynia,*
2 *chosen and destined by God the Father and*
*sanctified by the Spirit*
*for obedience to Jesus Christ and for sprinkling with his blood:*
*May grace and peace be multiplied to you.*

The *writer* is 'Peter' and his *position* is 'an apostle of Jesus Christ'. As an apostle Peter:

(i) was one of Christ's original followers (in fact, their leader);
(ii) saw the resurrected Christ (in fact, the first disciple to do so);
(iii) was given the Holy Spirit to have a God-given insight into Christ's coming, death and resurrection (in fact, Peter was the first post-resurrection preacher).

Although Peter is writing a general letter to be read to many people, his letter is personal, relevant and urgent. Later on he writes: 'So *I* exhort the elders among you, as a fellow elder and a witness of the sufferings of Christ...' (5:1). He repeatedly directs his words to 'you' ('...in this *you* rejoice' 1:6), so this is very much an 'I...you' letter. As modern day readers we still have a sense of the letter's immediacy.

The readers are scattered over a vast area, which today is known as the northern part of Turkey. The places mentioned were Roman provinces and Peter wrote the letter from 'Babylon', a coded reference to the capital of the empire, Rome (see 5:13). It is likely that Peter and Mark (also mentioned in 5:13) had travelled through this region at an earlier time before reaching 'Babylon'. Who brought Peter's letter to these remote places? Many think it was Silvanus (also known as Silas), who is mentioned later as Peter's amanuensis[4] (see 5:12), he was also a missionary colleague of Paul (see Acts 16:40-18:5 passim; 1 Thessalonians 1:1; 2 Corinthians 1:19).

Whoever it was, it appears he arrived from Rome to a port city in Pontus (on the southern coast of the Black Sea), making his way from church to church eastwards through Galatia to Cappadocia, then westwards to Asia completing his circuit in a port city in Bithynia (also on the Black Sea). Josephus, a Jewish historian of that era, referred to a similar itinerary (*Jewish Antiquities* 16.21-24), so perhaps he was following a well-known road system.

---

4. An 'amanuensis' was a scribe who wrote a letter either by direct dictation or with considerable freedom to put things 'in his own words'.

Peter's words to his readers are striking. He calls them *exiles of the dispersion*[5], that is, homeless stateless persons, people without a passport or any sense of belonging anywhere. Their situation was like the Karen people in South Asia, folk 'exiled' from their homeland and who are lifelong refugees. Peter is saying that their true homeland is heaven, from which they are (temporarily) 'dispersed' living as 'exiles' in various Roman provinces.

Then follows a truly remarkable contrast. In their present circumstances they are 'exiles', vulnerable and insecure, if it were not for their 'salvation ready to be revealed' (1:5) and that they are 'chosen and destined according to God the Father'(1:2). God, 'the father of the fatherless and the protector of widows' (Psalm 68:5), is truly their father. He has pre-determined that these poor homeless ones will be his children (see 1:17 – 'If you call him "Father"...'). If the readers are 'chosen by the Father', so too are those in 'Babylon', whom Peter calls 'likewise chosen' (5:13). It is no coincidence that the letter begins and ends on the note of God's choice of his people. In other words, whether in Asia Minor or Italy – these 'exiles' find their security in the Father's choice and calling of them.

It is obvious that in referring to 'the Father', 'the Spirit' and 'Jesus Christ' that Peter has the divine Trinity in mind (though he does not use the word). This is one of many passages in the New Testament where the three persons of the godhead are mentioned together. Usually the names are given in a specific order, that is, Father, Son and Holy Spirit. This is because the Father sent the Son who sent the Spirit (from the Father) and because the Spirit glorifies the Son who glorifies the Father. In other words, the Trinity of God is not to be thought of geometrically, like a heavenly triangle with equal sides. These 'Persons' are dynamically involved in working together in God's redemptive mission in the world.

---

5. A majority of Jews then lived outside their homeland Israel in 'the 'Dispersion' (Greek: diaspora). James' Letter is addressed to 'the twelve tribes of the Dispersion'.

That principle is to be found here in this text, despite the unusual order that places the Spirit second instead of third. Here it is important to notice Peter's use of those small but important words, prepositions. If their divine election is '*by* the Father', their 'sanctification' (or 'holiness') is '*by* the Spirit'. It is by means of the Spirit that these readers are able to lead holy lives. That, indeed, was God's intention in choosing and calling them. Just as their Father is 'holy', so too his children are to be 'holy' (1:16). It is not overstating the case to argue that one of Peter's main objectives in writing is to deepen their holiness and purity (see 1:14-18, 22).

Integrally connected is Peter's reference now to Jesus Christ. Once more the preposition is critical. They are chosen 'by the Father', 'by sanctification of the Spirit', '*for* obedience and sprinkling of the blood of Jesus Christ'. The end point of the Father's choice of them and the Spirit's sanctifying work, firstly, is that they *obey* Jesus Christ and secondly that they are *sprinkled* with his blood.

As his covenant people metaphorically 'sprinkled with his blood' they obey Jesus' teaching and follow his example. At Mt Sinai God gave his commandments and Moses sprinkled on the people with the blood of oxen as a sign that they had 'covenanted' to be God's special people (Exodus 24:8). Now, as it were, the blood of the crucified Jesus is (invisibly) sprinkled on them, signifying their forgiveness and that they are known as *his* people (of the New Covenant). The holiness of their lives, made possible *by* the Spirit, and by their obedience and imitation of Jesus, confirm this. Peter rounds off the introduction with the devout prayer (found also in Paul's letters), 'May grace and peace be multiplied to you'. Readers need to know that God acts towards us in grace and kindness and desires us to be at peace with him and with one another.

*Reflection on verses 1-2:* This raises a lot of issues and gives us plenty to think about. Do we recognise our fragility and vulnerability as 'exiles' in this present existence? Have we faced the humbling but comforting fact that we are believers and therefore secure only because the Father chose us to be his children? Are we quite clear that our Father's will and purpose for us is to be his 'holy' people and that the Holy Spirit is the source of the strength for that? Do we know that God's eternal purpose for us is that we obey and imitate Jesus, thereby demonstrating that we are indeed the people of Jesus, 'sprinkled with his blood'?

## THE BENEDICTION (1:3-9)

In synagogue meetings there were formal liturgies called 'Benedictions', in which those who gathered 'blessed' God. For example, *Benediction 1* (from the era of the New Testament) begins: '*Blessed* art thou, Lord our God and God of our fathers, God of Abraham, God of Isaac, God of Jacob...'.

In verses 3-9 Peter has 'christianised' this 'blessing' of God. Such was the impact of the *Son of God* on Peter that he changed his Jewish way of referring to God. Instead of blessing the God of 'our fathers' he has blessed the God who is 'the *Father* of our Lord Jesus Christ' and who, through Jesus, is also the *Father* of believers (see 1:3, 17).

Synagogue *Benediction 1* goes on to 'bless' God because he will fulfil his promises of 'grace' to the 'fathers' by bringing a 'redeemer', 'help' and 'salvation' to their 'children's' children'. First Peter shows that God's promises to Abraham, Isaac and Jacob have been fulfilled in the coming, death and resurrection of Christ and will be perfected at his 'revelation'. Note, for example, the prominence of 'salvation' in Peter's Benediction (verses 5 and 9) and the prominence of the idea of 'redemption' elsewhere in the letter (for example, 1:18 'You...were *ransomed*...with the precious blood of Christ').

3 *Blessed be the God and Father of our Lord Jesus Christ!*
*By his great mercy we have been born anew*
*to a living hope*
*through the resurrection of Jesus Christ from the dead, and*
4 *to an inheritance which is imperishable, undefiled, and unfading,*
*kept in heaven for you,*
5 *who by God's power are guarded through faith for a salvation*
*ready to be revealed in the last time.*

6 *In this you rejoice,*
*though now for a little while you may have to suffer various trials,*
7 *so that the genuineness of your faith,*
*more precious than gold which though perishable is tested by fire,*
*may redound to praise and glory and honor at the revelation of Jesus Christ.*
8 *Without having seen him you love him;*
*though you do not now see him you believe in him*
*and rejoice with unutterable and exalted joy.*
9 *As the outcome of your faith you obtain the salvation of your souls.*

Peter 'blesses' 'the God and Father of the Lord Jesus Christ' in verses 3-9. In brief, the Father has 're-birthed' believers giving them a 'living hope' for the 'inheritance' of their 'salvation' when Jesus Christ is 'revealed', a salvation in which they 'rejoice' despite the 'sufferings' of the present time which is refining their 'faith', to 'the glory of God'.

(i) The key idea in verses 3-9 is the Father's gift of 'living hope' to his children (verse 3). There are two levels of meaning here, one objective the other subjective. Objectively, there is the sure and certain 'hope' of 'life' beyond death in the kingdom of God, which Peter calls an 'inheritance' (verse 4) and 'salvation' (verses 5, 9). Subjectively, there is the 'liveliness' and urgency by which believers understand that 'hope'. The hope of life inspires a lively hope.

This 'living hope' is not the natural optimism some bright souls display regardless of the circumstances.[6] The Father 're-births' his people regardless of their innate optimism or pessimism giving them his *supernatural* gift of a 'living hope'. Here Peter is repeating Jesus' words to Nicodemus that he must be 'born again' (or, 'from above') before he can 'see' or 'enter' the Kingdom of God (John 3:3,7). God gives that 'authority' only to those who welcome his living Word, Jesus (John 1:12). James wrote something similar: 'Of [the Father's]

6. 'The optimist thinks this is the best of all possible worlds; the pessimist knows it' (J. Robert Oppenheimer, nuclear physicist).

own will he *gave us birth* (my translation) by the word of truth' (James 1:18). In other words, God himself 're-births' his children spiritually so that they are enlivened to have the sure hope of life beyond the grave.

Peter teaches that such supernatural re-birth has a basis and an instrument. Its *basis* is Jesus' own resurrection from the dead. Jesus' actual bodily resurrection is the foundation of the believer's resurrection and subsequent eternal life. We recollect Jesus' word, 'I am the resurrection and the life. He who believes in me, though he die, yet shall he live' (John 11:25). Without the resurrection of Christ there is no hope of eternal life. Thankfully, however, the resurrection of Jesus is a secure fact of history.

What, then, is the *instrument* by which God re-births his children to have this 'living hope'? It is the preaching of the Gospel. Soon Peter will write, 'You have been born anew...through the living and abiding word of God...the good news which was preached to you (1:23, 25).

(ii) Peter refers to this 'hope of life' in two other ways. First, he calls it 'an inheritance' (verse 4), like money or property left in a will. Peter, however, was recalling that God promised Abraham the land of Canaan as an 'inheritance' (Genesis 12:3) and which he gave to his people following the exodus. The people proved unworthy of God's kindness, however, and the land was subject to plague, famine and invasion. The people lost their inheritance because of their sinfulness. Peter, however, declares that believers' inheritance 'is imperishable, undefiled, and unfading, kept in heaven' for them (verse 4). God has chosen them by 'his great mercy' (verse 3) and 're-birthed' them; they will not lose what their merciful Father has promised them.

Peter also refers to this 'living hope' as 'salvation ready to be revealed in the last time' (verse 5; cf. verse 13—'at the revelation of Jesus Christ'). 'Reveal' and 'revelation' (in Greek, *apokalyptō, apokalypsis*) originally meant the 'removal of a veil'. In the New Testament it means the 'unveiling' of what will happen at the end of history. 'Salvation' is a medical word and meant the 'healing' of things that are currently diseased or broken. This 'hope' is secure since it is 'being guarded' by God until they enter it. When Peter says it is 'through faith' he does not mean that our faith is the means by which we have salvation. Rather, it is God who inspires faith in him as his Word, the gospel, is preached and heard.

(iii) That salvation, though 'at hand' (4:7) has not yet come but will be 'revealed in the last time' (verse 5) at 'the revelation of Jesus Christ' (verse 7). By this Peter means Jesus' second coming. In the meantime, however, life for them is precarious as they 'suffer various trials' (verse 6). This they 'must' do since following the Lord means bearing witness to him, regardless of the cost (3:15). As a result they are already suffering verbal abuse, social ostracism and probably some form of police action (2:12,18; 3:6,16; 4:4). Worse is to follow. Soon they will face a 'fiery' trial (4:12-19).

Perhaps Peter is anticipating that the persecutions of Nero (in which many Christians were burnt alive) will spread throughout the empire, reaching even those remote parts. Despite these sufferings, which are inevitable due to their identification with Christ, they 'rejoice with unutterable and exalted joy' (verse 8) at the prospect of their much hoped-for 'salvation'.

(iv) 'Faith' is important in Peter's 'blessing' of the Father. As noted above, their 'inheritance' is guarded for them by the power of God 'through faith' (verse 5). Peter speaks of the 'genuineness of faith' (verse 7), a metaphor for faith that is refined in the furnace of their sufferings, its impurities drawn off like dross from molten gold. After all, shallow or bogus faith is soon abandoned in the face of pain. The residue left behind by the fires of sufferings is a faith that brings glory to God since it is 'genuine' and obviously sincere. This 'faith' has an 'end' or 'goal' to which it is moving, the 'salvation of their souls' (verse 9). In this sense 'faith' is close in meaning to 'living hope' (verse 3).

Clearly, though, this 'faith' is deeply personal. It is

directed towards Jesus Christ who will be 'revealed' (verse 7) but whom they 'do not now see' (verse 8). Peter, witness to his sufferings (5:1), has indeed seen him but these readers have not seen him...yet. But they love him (verse 8) and walk in his footsteps (2:21).

*Reflection on verses 3-9:* Peter's beautiful eulogy inspires a reality check for us. Does the 'living hope' of the 'inheritance' of our coming 'salvation' burn brightly within us? Are we confident that it is being 'kept' and 'guarded' by God for us? Do we understand that because people rejected Christ, so they may also reject us, bringing a measure of suffering? Though we have not seen the Lord, as Peter had, do we nonetheless love him and truly believe in him?

People in antiquity felt deeply the tragedy of death. A section in the National Museum in Athens is dedicated to memorials for deceased loved ones. The Ilisos Stele presents a handsome young man (the deceased) who is being mourned by an old man (his father), a boy (his slave) and even his dog. The message of the gospel gives sure and certain confidence of a 'living hope' by the resurrection of Jesus. It is a wonderful and relevant message.

## SALVATION: PROPHESIED AND PROCLAIMED (1:10-12)

Peter has more to say about this 'living hope' (1:3), which is an incorruptible and secure 'inheritance' (1:4) and the 'salvation' now 'ready to be revealed' (1:5, 9). The prophets anticipated this 'salvation', and apostles and evangelists proclaimed it.

10 *The prophets who prophesied of the grace that was to be yours*
*searched and inquired about this salvation;*
11 *they inquired what person or time*
*was indicated by the Spirit of Christ within them*
*when predicting the sufferings of Christ and the subsequent glory.*
12 *It was revealed to them that they were serving not themselves but you,*
*in the things which have now been announced to you*
*by those who preached the good news to you*
*through the Holy Spirit sent from heaven,*
*things into which angels long to look.*

The word 'salvation', which comes at the end of the present translation in verse 10, actually comes at the beginning in Peter's original text and so picks up and continues the main theme of the previous passage.

(i) Peter says that the message of salvation involved a great sweep of history. This salvation was prophesied in the *past* ('prophets...searched and inquired' v10), has *now* been proclaimed to the readers ('by those who preached the good news' v12), and will be revealed in the *future* ('in the last time' 1:5). God has caught up readers (then and now) in his great activity that began centuries earlier with the prophets and will end sometime in the future with the 'revelation of Jesus Christ' (1:7).

(ii) This 'salvation' is centred in Jesus Christ. It was Christ who was prophesied back then; it is Christ who is being proclaimed now; it will be Christ who will be revealed at the last. Some years earlier Peter told the Supreme Council of the Jews in Jerusalem:

> There is salvation in no one else,
> for there is no other name under heaven given among men
> by which we must be saved (Acts 4:12).

Peter, leading disciple of Jesus, first witness of the resurrection and first preacher of the gospel is utterly convinced of the unique centrality of Jesus Christ for salvation.

(iii) Peter insists that this 'salvation' is located in 'the sufferings of Christ and the subsequent glory'. 'Christ' is Greek for the Hebrew word 'Messiah' or 'Anointed One', his special king who was to do his saving work for his chosen people. Jesus was his *name*, Christ was his *title,* and 'sufferings' and 'subsequent glory' was his *work* in achieving that salvation. Christ's 'sufferings' were sustained as he 'bore our sins in his body on the tree' (2:24) and his 'subsequent glory' occurred when 'God raised him from the dead and gave him glory' (1:21; cf. 4:11 'to him belong glory and dominion forever').

Suffering is a powerful theme in First Peter: '[a servant] suffering unjustly...patiently (2:19, 20); 'Christ suffered for you' (2:21); 'when he suffered, he did not threaten' (2:23); 'if you do suffer for righteousness' (3:14); 'better to suffer, for doing right' (3:17); 'Christ suffered for sins once' (3:18); 'Christ suffered in the flesh' (4:1); 'you share Christ's sufferings' (4:13); 'let none of you suffer as a...' (4:15); 'let those who suffer...entrust...' (4:19); '[Peter] a witness of the sufferings of Christ' (5:1); 'after you have suffered a little while' (5:10); 'knowing the same experience of suffering...' (5:8).

(iv) Peter acknowledges the indispensable role of the Holy Spirit in this Christ-centred salvation. We note that it was the 'Spirit of *Christ*' who was 'in' the prophets 'witnessing beforehand' to the 'sufferings' and 'glory' of *Christ*. In other words, Christ's own 'Spirit' (which is the Holy Spirit by another name) was prompting the prophets to 'search' and 'examine' as they sought to identify him, and the time when he was to come. The most prominent prophecies of those sufferings are Isaiah 53:4 and Deuteronomy 21:23, both of which are echoed later (see 2:21-25).

Furthermore, the same Spirit 'sent from heaven' was the means by which the 'good news' had been proclaimed in Pontus, Galatia, Cappadocia, Asia and Bithynia. By the Spirit God revealed his coming salvation to prophets and gave words about that salvation to apostles and evangelists. The Spirit is also the instrument of the 'holiness' that God wills for his people (1:2).

Who were 'those who preached the good news to you'? One possibility is that Jews from *Cappadocia, Pontus* and *Asia* (Acts 2:9) were among the 3000 on the Day of Pentecost who 'received Peter's word' and were baptised and instructed in the apostles teaching (Acts 2:41-42). Did these Jewish believers then return to their homeland preaching the gospel and forming churches there? Did Peter subsequently visit these believers in the churches northern Anatolia? This is the most likely explanation for Peter's extensive knowledge of these far-flung believers. Perhaps, too, Mark's greetings to them suggest that he, too, had visited these believers (5:13).

(v) This passage teaches that the central message of the Bible is about Christ, his 'sufferings' and 'glories'. The Old Testament prophesied Christ and the New Testament proclaims Christ. Angels, by contrast, only 'long to look' at the details about Christ that are made plain by prophets and preachers. In other words, even the angels of God do not know his purposes that are now revealed fully in the Bible.

The first disciples and the first generation of believers were Jews. However, they were in the minority. The majority of the people of Israel rejected Jesus as Messiah and, therefore, the witness of the prophets to him. This means that for God's historic people, the writings of the Old Testament remain incomplete, unfulfilled and ultimately mystifying. By contrast, those who welcome the good news about Christ, begin to understand the message of the prophets and indeed the whole Old Testament.

*Reflection on verses 10-12:* Christ's 'sufferings' and 'glories' is the message of the whole Bible, Old and New Testament. Prophets like Isaiah and Jeremiah had many important things to say in their generation, but ultimately they were foreshadowing the coming of Christ and the blessings of the salvation he brings to those who commit to him. In that sense, as Peter says, the prophets were 'not serving their own generation', but the generation of those who have come to believe. This remains true. Thus we read the whole Bible, as it were, through Christ-shaped glasses.

## BE HOLY (1:13-17)

The initial word 'therefore' indicates that the following teaching about behaviour arises directly from the previous passage. God has promised believers his salvation (1:3-9), *therefore* let the people 'be holy' (verse 16).

The exodus and the Mt Sinai covenant form the background to Peter's words. Earlier, the 'sprinkled blood' of Christ on his people (1:2) recalled Moses sprinkling blood of oxen on the people and the book of the covenant (Exodus 24:3-8). God had delivered them from Egypt and their solemn commitment to keep his requirements marked them as his people, signified by the 'sprinkled blood'.

In the passage following Peter continues to think about God's earlier parallel action in saving the people from Egypt and the response he required from them. At Mt Sinai he commanded the people he had saved, 'Be holy, as I the Lord your God am holy' (Leviticus 19:2). There is an integral connection between God's merciful action and the response of holiness he requires. That is as true of God's ultimate action under the New Testament as it was under the Old.

13 *Therefore gird up your minds,*
*be sober,*
*set your hope fully upon the grace that is coming to you*
*at the revelation of Jesus Christ.*
14 *As obedient children, do not be conformed to the passions of your former ignorance,*
15 *but as he who called you is holy, be holy yourselves in all your conduct;*
16 *since it is written, 'You shall be holy, for I am holy.'*
17 *And if you invoke as Father*
*him who judges each one impartially according to his deeds,*
*conduct yourselves with fear throughout the time of your exile.*

Three commands in this passage can be summed up in the words 'hope', 'be holy' and 'fear'.

(i) Peter first enjoins 'hope' for the 'coming grace' that is being brought to them at the 'revelation of Jesus Christ' (verse 13). The key idea of 'revelation' (Greek *apokalypsis*) is of unveiling or uncovering something that was hidden from sight. (See also 1:5,7,12; 4:13; 5:1.) Here the picture unusually is of that 'grace' being brought *to* us, rather than of us moving towards it.

We recall that Peter 'blessed' God for 're-birthing' believers to a 'living hope' (1:3). As with other good things that God inspires within us, it is appropriate for us to respond with hope to God's mercy.

Clearly this is a very serious hope that is (a) carefully thought out ('gird up the loins of your minds' is based on the practice of workmen tucking their outer garments into their underclothes); (b) 'sober' (not erratic); and (c) 'mature' (not childish).

One way of stirring up this God-given hope is to reflect upon the basis of that hope, that is, upon the historicity of the resurrection of Jesus Christ from the dead (1:3). The evidence for this is secure. If it is not then Christianity is at best based on a woeful misunderstanding, or at worst on a monumental hoax. On the contrary, Jesus' resurrecting from the dead gives us solid grounds for believing that he will be 'revealed' at the end of history, ushering in the day of salvation and bringing our 'inheritance' to us.

(ii) Peter's, 'Be holy'[7] is the positive part of a longer injunction that begins with the negative, 'do not be conformed to the passions of your former ignorance' (verses 14-16). Their 'former ignorance' means their ignorance about God before they were 're-birthed' to a living hope (1:3), that is, before the good news was preached to them (1:12, 25). Later Peter will remind them that they were 'ransomed from the futile ways inherited from your fathers' (1:18), which included sexual carousing and idol worship (4:3). Evidently some of Peter's readers were Gentiles, since Jews of that era would not have behaved this way.

'Passions of former ignorance' is strong language for their settled way of life before they became believers. 'Passions' translates the idea of 'burning desire' (cravings) that carries with it almost the idea of addiction. These vices had them in a 'prison' from which they were unable and indeed unwilling to be free.

---

7. 'Holy' is God's own description of his character ('I, the Lord your God, am holy...'). Holiness denotes God's utter moral and spiritual purity and perfection that distinguishes God from man the sinner ('Thus says the high and lofty one who inhabits eternity, whose name is holy, "I dwell in the high and holy place..."' Isaiah 57:15).

We remember that God gave the redeemed Hebrews his 'Holiness Code' at Mt Sinai (Leviticus 17-26). They were not to follow the practices of the Egyptians behind them nor of the Canaanites ahead of them (Leviticus 18:1-5). On the contrary, they were to be God's holy people because he, the LORD who had rescued them was holy (Leviticus 19:2 – 'You shall be holy; for I the LORD your God am holy'; 20:26 – 'You shall be holy to me, for I the LORD am holy, and have separated you from the peoples that you should be mine').

Leviticus' 'Holiness Code' went into precise detail about unholiness and uncleanness. Peter is more general at this point (though he will say more throughout the letter). Here he merely says, 'Be holy *in all your conduct*' (verse 15). 'Conduct' translates a Greek word that Peter uses extensively in this letter. Literally it meant 'turn upside down' and as used by Peter may still point to the revolutionary nature of the new life associated with holy living. RSV's 'conduct' sounds rather moralistic (like doing your 'good deed for the day'), but Peter's word is far more radical and all embracing than that.

The parallel is clear. God has mercifully rescued this people from bondage to sin and enjoined holiness upon them just as he had rescued the Hebrews from bondage in Egypt and enjoined holiness on them. There are differences, yet the pattern of divine redemption followed by the divine command for holiness is the same because God is the same.

One significant difference is that the covenant LORD of the Old Covenant is now revealed as 'Father'. Under the former covenant God was occasionally referred to as the covenant 'Father' of the people, in a global sense. There are relatively few Old Testament references to God as 'father' of the nation (see for example Deuteronomy 32:6; Isaiah 63:16; 64:8; Jeremiah 3:4, 19; 31:9; Malachi 1:6; 2:10). Under the New Covenant that global sense continues but is intensely personal. He is 'Father' to each believer. This new reality is made possible by each believer's connection with the one true Son of God, Jesus. Through that Son, and the indwelling presence of the Spirit of his Son, we are now sons and daughters of God by adoption (see Romans 8:15-17, 23; cf. Galatians 4:6). Jesus taught the sons and daughters of God to articulate their relationship with the Father in the Lord's Prayer (as noted below).

It is easy to miss Peter's reference to the Father's 'call' to believers (verse 15). The Father who has chosen them (1:2) has 'called' them to be his children through those who have preached the Gospel to them (1:12; cf. 1:25). The Father 'calls' men and women to belong to his Son so that through him they become children of God. At its heart the message of the Gospel is deeply relational.

At the beginning of the letter Peter taught that believers are 'sanctified by the Spirit' whereas here he instructs *them*, 'be holy'. Just as 'hope' is God's regenerating act in us (1:3) *and* something we stir ourselves to have (1:14), likewise holiness is ours by his Spirit (1:2) *as well as* something which we must fulfil. Hope and holiness are coins with two sides. They are God's gifts *and* our responsibility.

The connection between God's mercy and his holiness is fundamental. The assurance of salvation that is kept in heaven and guarded by God (1:3-4) does not remove our obligation to live holy lives. This principle also emerges in the next injunction.

(iii) Peter's third injunction is to call on his readers to 'fear' God. This is because their 'Father' upon whom they 'call' (as in the Lord's Prayer, 'Father, hallowed be thy name...') is also their judge. This Father, who has chosen and re-birthed them (1:2,3), will also judge them. Sounding very like Paul, Peter declares that the Father will 'impartially judge the work of each' (cf. Romans 2:6, 11 '[God] will render to every man according to his works...God shows no partiality'). Note that the Father who is our impartial judge is also 'holy' (verse 16).

People rightly ask, how are we to 'fear' God when he is 'our Father' who loves us and whom we are to love? To 'fear God' is to have a deep respect for him that does not take him for granted, and that understands the dire consequences of knowingly turning away from him. Above all, the 'fear' of God recognises the awesome cost of our redemption, that is, by the blood of his own Son (see 1:19; Romans 8:32). Analogies are always flawed, but think for example of the Grand Canyon that inspires 'awe' at its magnificence, but also a healthy 'fear' of falling from its great height. We stand in awe at God's almightiness and holiness and 'fear' the consequences of disobeying him. At the human level, a child will love a good father, but also 'fear' the consequences of offending him in some way.

*Reflection on verses 13-17:* It is not clear from the Bible how God will judge our works when he is also our gracious saviour. Nonetheless, the apostles teach both realities so it is vital that we hold to both. Having said that, the dominant truth is that God is gracious and loving and Christ's death and resurrection has abundantly secured our salvation. Peter and Paul do not teach about our accountability to God in order to sow seeds of doubt about that salvation, but to stir us to act responsibly towards God. The recurring refrain of the Wisdom Literature is that the 'fear of the Lord is the beginning of knowledge' and that 'fools despise wisdom' (see for example, Proverbs 1:7).

This is likely the point Peter is making here. He does not want his readers to be 'shaped by' their bad old ways. When the Father 'called' them through the Gospel and 're-birthed' them to a 'living hope' they drew a line (at baptism) under 'the passions of their former ignorance', determined to leave them behind.

## RANSOMED (1:18-21)

In this letter Peter often gives his teaching in a short paragraph like this one. Frequently he uses linking words to pick up and carry forward key ideas from earlier paragraphs, in this case, it is the word 'knowing'. In the original text 'knowing' actually belongs to the previous sentence, and should be preceded by a comma not a full stop. A more precise translation would be: '...conduct yourselves with fear throughout the time of your exile, *knowing*...', meaning the fear we are to feel will be explained by what we 'know'.

Meanwhile, we note that his words 'you were ransomed...with ...blood...of a lamb' (verses 18-19) echo the first Passover in Egypt, which was the prelude to and means of the Hebrews' escape from slavery. Clearly the entire passage springs from and is inspired by the Exodus.

There is a repeating typology here.

Then the prison was physical, Egypt. Now the 'prison' is moral and spiritual, 'the futile ways inherited from your fathers' (verse 18). Then God rescued his people under the shed blood of the Passover Lamb. Now God rescues his people by the 'sprinkled blood' (1:2) of the spotless 'lamb' of God, Christ. Then God bound the people to himself by their agreement to be holy, though that holiness was often expressed ritually as well as morally. Now God binds the people to himself by their commitment to holiness that is entirely moral and ethical. Then God rescued his people for life in the 'promised land' of Canaan, which they lost through their own folly. Now God rescues them for an 'inheritance' that cannot be corrupted or lost.

By recapitulating these saving acts, though on a bigger and broader canvas, God has revealed his essential character as a redeemer of the imprisoned and saviour of the lost.

As well as looking backwards Peter's 'knowing that' also points forwards. What is it that we 'know'? Apostolic writers often use the words 'knowing' or 'we know' to remind the readers of teachings that they have come to 'know' by previous instruction. They appeal to readers' memory. Peter's words here, in fact, are rather creed-like. They mention Christ's pre-existence, his coming into the world, his redemptive death, his resurrection and his present 'glory'. It is not hard to see how passages like this inspired the next generations of Christian leaders to develop statements of belief like the Apostles Creed.

Peter is not merely rehearsing a sequence of items about Christ that might only engage the mind. By no means! He wants readers to 'know' what they know for two important reasons. First, that they 'fear' the Father (1:17), because the cost of their redemption from slavery was 'the blood' of the spotless Christ. Second, that this Christ who died was resurrected and glorified to give them 'hope', a hope with a real and substantial basis through the resurrection of Jesus from the dead. Here he picks up the theme of 'living hope' from the beginning of the letter (1:3). In short, this is information about Christ that inspires rightful 'fear' on one hand, and 'living hope' on the other.

1:18 *You know that you were ransomed*
*from the futile ways inherited from your fathers,*
*not with perishable things such as silver or gold,*
1:19 *but with the precious blood of Christ,*
*like that of a lamb without blemish or spot.*
1:20 *He was destined before the foundation of the world*
*but was made manifest at the end of the times for your sake.*
1:21 *Through him you have confidence in God,*
*who raised him from the dead and gave him glory,*
*so that your faith and hope are in God.*

Four observations come out of this powerful and deeply moving passage:

(i) Readers past and present need to 'know' at what great price the Father purchased their freedom. Under the Old Covenant it was the blood of the Passover lambs. Under the New Covenant it is the blood of a man, that is, of God's anointed king, Jesus the Christ.

Previously they had been enslaved to 'the passions of…former ignorance' (1:14), the 'futile ways inherited from…fathers' (verse 18). Parents passed on to their children generation upon generation a culture of bondage, from which they have now been set free.

They have not merely 'turned over a new leaf', having resolved to live differently. Rather, they are now free because God has set them free from their moral and spiritual prison. This freedom, however, did not come cheaply but at unimaginable cost to God.

The 'living hope' is for an '*incorruptible* inheritance' (1:3-4), which means that the 'price of release' from this present moral prison must likewise be *incorruptible*. At that time and today we place huge store by 'silver and gold'. Yet these apparently precious items are 'corruptible', and easily lost through theft, inflation, taxation and misadventure. Silver and gold could never purchase the redemption of the imprisoned human soul.[8]

Rather, 'the precious blood of Christ, like that of a lamb without blemish or spot' (verse 19) was the incorruptible 'price' that was paid to release us from the grip of sin. Once more the underlying Egypt-Mt Sinai-Canaan typology comes to the surface. Just as the Passover lamb must be unblemished as a sacrifice for the release of the Hebrews (Exodus 12:5), so must the Lamb of God be unblemished for his greater sacrifice. The imagery of Christ the Passover sacrifice runs through the New Testament (John 1:29; 1 Corinthians 5:7; Revelation 5:6).

Peter will speak later about Christ's moral perfection, 'he committed no sin. No guile was found on his lips' (2:22). The apostles knew that Christ's sinlessness was the necessary qualification for him to be the sin bearer (see for example, 2 Corinthians 5:21; Hebrews 5:9; 7:26-27; 9:14).

By using the word 'redeem' Peter is employing the language of 'the price of release' for a prisoner of war, a slave or a debtor. The word 'redeem' may derive from Jesus' famous saying about 'giving his life a ransom for many' (Mark 10:45). In that world slaves were bought and sold like cattle. Occasionally, a third party would pay a slave owner the 'redemption' price for the freedom of a slave. While this language would have been meaningful for the slaves among Peter's readers (see 2:18-20), it is more likely that he is thinking of the Lord's redemption of his *people* from slavery in Egypt.

---

8. Peter often uses the word 'soul' (psyche - 1:9, 22; 2:11, 25; 4:19), though not in the Greek sense of the disembodied 'soul' that survives death. Rather, Peter is thinking of the Hebrew idea of 'soul' as the whole living *embodied* person (Hebrew: nephesh).

(ii) Because his readers 'know' the incalculable cost of their redemption (verses 18-19), they 'fear' their Father (1:17) who has paid such a price for it.

That redemption affects every aspect of daily life. They have been 'redeemed out of the empty manner of life handed over by their fathers' (verse 18). This paints a grim picture of fathers 'handing over' to their children a 'futile' way of living. Peter describes these later as freewheeling sexual practices, drinking bouts and idol worship (see 4:2-3). The Graeco-Roman world of the time was, like ours in the west, sexually debased, plagued with alcoholism and gambling, preoccupied with entertainment, accepting of abortion and suicide. It was a decadent era, and an age of anxiety overshadowed by the omnipresent reality of death.

For re-birthed believers, however, this bondage lay in the past. Preachers have come and told them of God's redemptive love in the Messiah, Jesus (1:12). They have been regenerated, 'born again' by the living and abiding word of the Gospel (1:3, 25). They have the assurance that their past sins have been cleansed (1:22) by the precious blood of Christ (verse 19) and the sure prospect of an incorruptible inheritance based on the resurrection of Jesus Christ from the dead (1:3-4). They have been rescued out of a futile and hopeless past so they must no longer be 'shaped by it' (1:14) and they must respect the possibility of being drawn back into it (1:17). True, the Father has 'chosen' and 'called' them through his gracious word. Yet they must not take him for granted, nor underestimate the enticements of the old demons.

(iii) Peter takes the opportunity to enlarge their view of Christ:

> He was foreknown before the foundation of the world,
> being made manifest at the end of times...
> God...raised him from the dead, and
> gave him glory.

Peter provides a majestic, sweeping summary of Christ's 'story' from eternity ('before the foundation of the world') to eternity ('glory'), with his redemptive foray within human history (his initial coming, his death, his resurrection). One feels very small beneath this Christ who overarches us.

Christ was 'foreknown' (by God), 'made manifest' (by God), 'raised' (by God) and 'given glory' (by God). Peter knew firsthand that Jesus knew he was 'sent' by God and that he was not a free agent. Jesus was submissive to the Father's will, whether as he faced Satan's temptations, or in the agony of the Garden of Gethsemane or in his sense of abandonment on the cross. Wherever we see Jesus he is doing not his own will but the will of him who sent him.

As noted above, Peter's 'story' of Christ informed and inspired Christians in the coming centuries to write creeds as the basis of Church life. The longest section of those various creeds was devoted to Christ's 'story'. Much of the New Testament is dedicated to telling that overarching story, in part or in whole. The Prologue of the Gospel of John tells that narrative from pre-creation to Incarnation (John 1:1-18), whereas in Romans 8:34 Paul tells it from Christ's death to his exaltation, and in Hebrews from the sufferings of his life through to his intercessions in heaven (Hebrews 2:10-18). These are just some of many statements of this kind.

This is God's Christ. This is our king and our saviour.

(iv) All that is true of Christ and his overarching story is, Peter said, 'for' them (that is believers). He was made manifest 'for' his people and he was raised alive and glorified so that they might have a sure faith and a certain hope in God.

This summary of Christ is not merely to tell a 'story' that we passively believe. Its purpose is that we will actively believe in God and have a 'living hope' in the coming incorruptible inheritance.

*Reflection on 1:18-21:* This short passage (verses 18-21) is powerful. Peter tells us the reason we 'fear' the Father who judges is the high price the Father paid for our deliverance from a hopeless life. Only an incorruptible sacrifice could win an incorruptible inheritance. As redeemed out of the 'Egypt' of a hope-less lifestyle, let readers past and present not slip back from where, by the grace of God, they have now been set free.

## RE-BORN (1:22-2:3)

At first sight this passage appears to be an independent, freestanding mini-sermon within the letter. When we look more closely we see Peter picking up key teachings that he has already introduced:

| | |
|---|---|
| 'born again' | 1:3 |
| 'imperishable' | 1:4, 18 |
| 'preaching the gospel' | 1:12 |
| 'salvation' | 1:5, 9, 10 |

Furthermore, his apparently clinching statement, 'for you have tasted the kindness of the Lord' proves not to be his last word, but leads into a new section (2:4) beginning, 'having come to him' (that is, 'the Lord').

There are also new teachings, which are both theological and ethical. The *theological* ones are 'purified by obedience' and 'tasted the kindness of the Lord', and the *ethical* ones are 'love one another' and 'put off all malice and all guile and insincerity and envy and all slander'. Congregational life is the place where these ethical imperatives are worked out. Positively, we are to love one another in the church and negatively we are to put off all forms of malice towards one another in that fellowship.

Briefly, we must note Peter's method of emphasising the 'imperishable' nature of God's salvation (redemption and re-birth). He does this by a 'not...but' comparison in verses 18-19 (for redemption) and also in verse 23 (for re-birth).

| | |
|---|---|
| ...you were ransomed from...futile ways... | You have been born again |
| not with perishable things such as silver or gold, | not of perishable seed |
| but with the precious blood of Christ | but of imperishable, |
| | through the living and abiding word of God |

The effect of denial followed by affirmation is powerful and demonstrates the absolute nature of God's salvation. Neither redemption nor re-birth can be secured by human effort; these come only from God.

22 *Having purified your souls by your obedience to the truth*
*for a sincere love of the brethren,*
*love one another earnestly from the heart.*
23 *You have been born again,*[9]
*not of perishable seed but of imperishable,*
*through the living and abiding word of God;*
24 *for 'All flesh is like grass and all its glory like the flower of grass.*
*The grass withers, and the flower falls,*
25 *but the word of the Lord abides for ever.'*
*That word is the good news which was preached to you.*
1 *So put away all malice and all guile and insincerity and envy*
*and all slander.*
2 *Like newborn babes, long for the pure spiritual milk,*
*that by it you may grow up to salvation;*
3 *for you have tasted the kindness of the Lord.*

Let me streamline Peter's teaching here in two broad statements, each of which is not an end in itself, but has *an expected outcome.*

| | | |
|---|---|---|
| v22 | You have purified your souls | *for* love of one another. |
| v23 | You have been born again | *so* (a) put off evil practices and (b) grow towards salvation. |

(i) 'Purified' (verse 22). Although Peter says 'you have purified your souls' he does not mean that people purify themselves. God cleanses the human soul from sins. What we are to do is 'obey the truth', that is, the 'truth' of 'the word of the Lord' (soon to be mentioned in v25). That 'truth' once obeyed brings *God's* cleansing of the soul. Paul wrote in similar terms to the Ephesians that 'Christ loved the church and gave

9. RSV has 'born anew', as in 1:3.

himself up for her, that he might sanctify her, having *cleansed* her *by* the washing of water with *the word*' (Eph 5:26).

Peter's words 'purified', like 'sanctified' (1:2), recall the Pharisees' obsessive concerns for the ritual purity of the people. Remember their clash with Jesus because his disciples did not practise the ritual washing of hands before re-entering the house after shopping in the marketplace (Mark 7:1-5; cf. John 2:6)? This was self-achieved purity that had to be maintained by keeping a veritable forest of legalistic requirements. Peter referred to these endless rules as, 'a yoke...which neither our fathers nor we have been able to bear' (Acts 15:10). By striking contrast Peter says that believers have been purified 'for unhypocritical[10] love'.

As a Jew Peter had lived in a deeply religious society that was marked by 'hypocrisy'. The word 'hypocrite' had its origin in the theatre for 'playacting' from which it evolved into religious 'hypocrisy', ungodliness hiding behind a mask of piety. Jesus used the work 'hypocrite' as a metaphor for the Pharisees' 'play acting', putting on an outward show of piety.

The Pharisees created numerous complicated rules and they lived in ways that were often judgmental and harsh (see for example, their verdict on the ordinary people in John 7:49: 'This crowd who do not know the law are accursed.') Accordingly, they loved neither God, nor neighbour. By contrast, Jesus summed up our duty to God as two great commandments, to love God and to love neighbour. That is the 'easy yoke' and 'light burden' Jesus gives to those who accepted his gracious invitation to 'come to him for rest' (Matthew 11:28-30).

Peter perfectly summed up his Lord's teaching. People are purified through obeying the Gospel not by performing outward rituals and this God-given purity issues in loving one's neighbour. Christ's new community of purified people is to be

---

10. Greek anhypokriton literally means 'unhypocritical'. RSV's bland rendering 'sincere' misses the point Peter is making, which is to reject 'hypocrisy' and express 'fervent love' to others.

characterised by 'unhypocritical brotherly love', something that had not usually been true of the Pharisee-led synagogues.

Sadly, nor is it always true of churches despite Peter's injunction, 'love one another earnestly from the heart'.

For three years Peter had lived with eleven other disciples as they sat at the feet of Jesus their teacher. He repeatedly taught them to love and serve one another in all humility (Mark 9:33-37; 10:35-45). Equally he gave them an example of that love in washing their feet, an act of service that pointed to his great act of love in dying to cleanse them from sins (John 13:10). On that occasion, Jesus said 'If I then, your Lord and Teacher, have washed your feet, you also ought to wash one another's feet' (John 13:14).

This is not Peter's last word on love within the fellowship of believers. Soon he will expand upon this important theme (4:7-11). Furthermore, his list of items to 'put off' (2:1) show in practical ways that the positive we call 'love' is expressed in avoiding all forms of the negative we call 'malice'.

(ii) 'Born again' (verse 23). Verse 23 does not begin a new sentence,[11] but continues on from verse 22 so that it reads, 'love one another...*because* you have been born again'. God is now their 'Father' and they, his children, are brothers and sisters in the family of God where 'family affection' is to be the mark of their relationships.

(a) Peter's 'because you have been born again' (verse 23) picks up 'we have been born again' from the beginning of the letter (1:3). When we combine these two references we notice three important aspects of this 're-birth'.

First, it is God who re-births us as his sons or daughters. God is now 'Father' to those he 're-births'. If our human parents 'generate' us as their children, then God our Father '*re*generates' us as *his* children. This he does so that we 'know' him, which we do as we pray to him as 'our Father...'.

---

11. As in RSV.

Second, our Father 're-births' us individually, but also as brothers and sisters in his family. Accordingly, we are to 'love one another with family affection', as noted above.

Third, our Father has 're-birthed' us to have a 'living hope' (1:3) of an 'inheritance' that is 'imperishable' (1:4). Each of us will die, yet as children of God we have the sure expectation of life beyond death in the kingdom of God. The basis of our certain 'hope' is Jesus Christ, his redemptive death for us (1:18) and his resurrection from the dead (1:3).

It is important that we engage in a reality check. Do we actively call on God our Father in prayer? Are we actively loving and serving our brothers and sisters in the family of God? Do we have a 'living hope' of an 'imperishable' inheritance, kept in heaven for us?

(b) This prompts the question as to how the Father makes us his children. Peter makes it clear that God 're-births' us by an 'imperishable seed', which is 'the living and abiding word of God' (verse 23).

We must note Peter's contrast between things that 'perish' (or 'become corrupt') and those that are 'imperishable' (or 'unable to be corrupted'). The Hebrews' 'inheritance' of Canaan was 'perishable', as indeed it proved to be, through locust plagues and foreign invaders. By contrast, the heavenly inheritance is 'imperishable', 'incorruptible' (1:4). Likewise, Peter wrote that the believers' redemption was not purchased by 'corruptible' items like silver or gold, but only by means of the 'incorruptible' price of the blood of Jesus the unblemished 'lamb' of God (1:18-19).

Consistent with an imperishable inheritance and an imperishable redemption Peter now points to the 'imperishable seed' that the Father sows in men and women to make them his children.

In verse 24 Peter skilfully quotes from Isaiah the prophet (Isaiah 40:6-9) to distinguish 'perishable' flesh from God's 'imperishable word'. Peter's portrayal of Mediterranean climate tells us how 'perishable' our human life is. The grass is green and the flowers grow in winter and spring, but quickly become brown and withered with the scorching blasts of summer heat. Humanity is, indeed, 'flesh' that displays its 'glory' for a brief season. But then the dry winds of ageing and death come and its beauty is no more. Walk around a graveyard and be reminded of the brevity of human 'glory' and tell yourself that this, too, is true of you!

In sharp contrast Peter declares that the 'word of the Lord abides forever' and is an 'imperishable seed' (verses 25a, 23). 'Abide' is rather an old fashioned word—the Greek *(menō)* simply means 'remain' or 'continue'. In other words, God's Word takes its character from God himself. The word is life-giving because it is the living word of the living God.

So it is by means of this 'imperishable word' that the Father re-births 'perishable' people to become his children whose 'living hope' is for an 'imperishable inheritance'.

(c) What is this 'word' that can give 'life' to ageing and dying humanity? Peter leaves to the end his dramatic disclosure that it is 'the word which was preached to you' (verse 25b). This 'word' that is 'preached' is the Gospel-word, the good news about Jesus Christ. This picks up Peter's earlier reference (1:12) to 'those who preached the good news to you' (literally, 'those who *gospelled* you').

Are we able to discover the words that these first evangelists would have used? Peter's first chapter in his letter allows us to hear echoes of that early preaching, in particular, verses 10-12. The Greek (*to euangelisthen*) makes clear that it is not preaching in general, but Gospel-preaching. This 'gospelling' focused on 'the sufferings and subsequent glory' of Christ, in fulfilment of the prophets' words, that called for a decisive act of personal commitment to Christ, determined to leave behind the evils of the past.

(d) Re-birth is not an end in itself any more than biological birth is an end in itself (verse 1). Soon after a baby is born the hospital will give careful instruction about the nourishment and care of the child. Once at home parents will take their child to special clinics for further advice during those early weeks and months. As the baby grows into a toddler the parents will establish and reinforce various boundaries for acceptable behaviour.

There is a sense in which Peter follows this principle in the passage (1:22-2:3), with one significant difference. These readers are new believers who, it appears, were baptised after living for some or even many years as unbelievers. They easily bring the behaviour of their past life into their newly re-born life. We remember his words about 'passions of former ignorance' (1:14) and 'futile ways inherited from your fathers' (1:18).

Re-birth does not in itself wipe away past attitudes and activities. With God's help (and the help of friends) we must leave a number of things behind. Here Peter speaks of 'putting off', as if referring to irreparably soiled and contaminated clothing.

Therefore, casting off

| | | |
|---|---|---|
| | all | malice, |
| and | all | guile, |
| and | | hypocrisies,[12] |
| and | | envy, |
| and | all | slander. |

None of these evils are 'physical', like some of those mentioned later (4:15). Rather, these are subtle sins. 'Malice' is a hostile attitude towards another person that seeks opportunity to do harm. 'Guile' conveys the idea of half-truths and other means of manipulation. 'Hypocrisy' is that rank error of religious people whose public piety masks private evil. 'Envy' is a fundamental discontent where we are jealous of the circumstances and gifts of others; sometimes 'envy' is acted out as 'malice'. 'Slander' is speaking (or writing) untruthfully about others, so as to blacken their name; sometimes 'slander' arises from 'envy'.

---

12. RSV has 'insincerity' despite Greek 'hypocrisies' (hypokriseis). See 1:22.

This 'vice' list coming so soon after the injunction 'love one another' (1:22) suggests a connection between the two. It seems likely that these evils are concrete examples of a lack of love. Indeed, it appears that the list of evils relate in particular to life *within* the Christian community. It is as if Peter is telling them that they will suffer some of these evils from outsiders (see for example, 2:12; 3:13-17), so let them not treat one another in those ways.

(e) Rather, Peter urges them along another path (verse 2).

> As newly born babes,
> long for the pure, spiritual milk,
> that by it you may grow up to salvation,
> for you have tasted the kindness of the Lord.

'Newly born babes' suggests that Peter's readers are recently 'born again', through the Gospel-word that was preached to them (1:12, 25).

Peter does not identify this 'milk' though there is little doubt as to his meaning. The context has been about being 'born again' by the 'Gospel-word' (1:12, 25). This word assured them of the 'kindness of the Lord'. Accordingly, that 'milk' which is 'pure' and 'spiritual'[13] is the message of the Gospel.

Here, though, such milk is not to be equated with the mere basics of the Gospel. For all practical purposes Peter is pointing to his letter as the 'milk' that will bring salvation growth. This letter teaches both the blessings of the Gospel, but also its responsibilities, including under persecution. Its original readers would have grown into mature Christians by acting out the teaching of this letter in the dire circumstances they faced.

(f) Peter concludes this passage with a quotation from Psalm 34:8, which originally said: 'Taste and see that the

13. Greek (to logikon) is much debated. Most likely it signals something that is not literal but metaphorical, as it were. Hence: 'long for the pure milk, figuratively speaking'.

Lord is good.' Peter slightly changes the command to the observation, '*for* you have tasted the kindness of the Lord'. His readers, having been evangelised, have been 'born again', 'redeemed' from a futile way of life and 'purified'. In other words, they *have already* 'tasted' that the Lord is good.

Here, the 'Lord' must be understood as the *Lord Jesus Christ.* This is quite remarkable since the original Psalm was referring to the Lord God of Israel. In short, Peter is identifying Jesus with Yahweh, and accordingly ascribing deity and divine majesty to him.

When Peter quotes the Psalm saying that 'the Lord is good' we should note a likely wordplay or pun. 'Good' translates the Greek *chrēstos*, which is identical with the word *Christos* (Christ) apart from one vowel. In Matthew 11:30 Jesus invited the weary to come to him and to take his yoke which, he said, was *chrēstos* (kind). Moreover, Peter's letter reflects the new freedom of his readers from the slavery of their previous way of living (1:14, 18). They have, indeed, 'tasted' that the Lord (Jesus) is 'kind'. It is as if the early Christians were saying *Christos* is *chrēstos* (kind).

In this passage, 1:22 –2:3, Peter has woven together an intricate verbal tapestry. But his aim was not to impress us with his artistry. Rather, it was to drive home the never-to-be-broken connection between (a) what God does for us, and (b) our necessary response. One idea leads into the next so that the whole life of the believer is a connected whole.

So the passage works like this:

God has purified you?
*Then* love one another.
You love one another?
It is *because* you have been born again by God's word.
You have been born again?
*Then* put away all evil and grow to full adulthood.
You are growing up?
It is *because* you have tasted the kindness of the Lord.

Like the good fisherman he was, Peter will not let us off the hook. We must conduct ourselves according to God's requirements; and those requirements are only possible because of what God has done.

*Reflection on 1:22-2:3:* This is an intricately woven passage that teaches us many important things about the Christian life. God has wiped away our sins, and we are to live in loving relationships within the family of believers. This 'love' in turn arises from the Father's 're-birthing' of his children and occurs through the imperishable Gospel-word. As newly born babes, believers are to 'put off' the evils of their former lives and seek to grow towards salvation by obeying the pure teaching of the word (set out in this letter).

## NEW TEMPLE, NEW PRIESTHOOD (2:4-10)

Peter does not use the word 'church' in this letter. Nonetheless, the injunction to 'love one another' (1:22) and later references to congregational life (see on 4:7-11) and the role of 'elders' (5:1-4) leave us in no doubt that church life was fundamental to these readers. Likewise, the present passage about 'new temple' and 'new priesthood' is focused on meetings of believers, though without the explicit 'church' terminology we find, for example, in Paul's letters.

There is an important connection with the previous passage about being 'born again' (verse 23) as a 'newly born babe' (verse 2) who has 'tasted that the Lord is kind' (verse 3) and who has 'come to him' (verse 4). For, when one 'comes to' Christ, one is also to be 'built into a spiritual house' (verse 5). I am 'born again' into God's family where I am nurtured and grow, loving others and being loved.

Peter makes quite clear that Christ is the 'stone' upon which the 'spiritual' temple-house is built. Indeed, 'stone' is the key word in the passage where it appears in three Old Testament quotations. Jesus quoted Psalm 118:22 referring to *himself* as 'the stone' the builders (the temple hierarchy) rejected which was to become 'the corner-stone' of the new temple of God (Mark 12:10; cf. Acts 4:11). To Jesus' 'stone' citation Peter has added two others (Isaiah 8:14; 28:16) to form a 'chain' of references. For those who 'believe' in him the 'stone' is 'precious' and becomes their life's foundation (verse 7a). For those who disbelieve, however, Christ is the 'stone' against whom they 'stumble', to their eternal destruction (verse 7b).

This passage continues the 'new Israel' theme that has run beneath Peter's text throughout. Peter re-narrates Israel's 'story' in an elaborate and sustained way. The Father 'chose' these 'exiles' whom he 'redeemed' from 'out of' slavery (Egypt) by means of the 'precious blood of Christ' (Passover lamb) so that he 'sprinkled them with blood' and demanded they 'be holy' (in a new covenant, as at Mt Sinai) whereupon he gave them their 'inheritance' (Canaan). To this narrative Peter now adds that they are a 'house' (that is the Temple), and a 'priesthood' offering 'sacrifices acceptable to God'. Furthermore, they are his 'chosen race', his 'holy nation', and his 'own people'. Just as God intended Israel to be his 'light to the nations' (Isaiah 49:6) so, too, the people of Jesus Christ are to be God's 'light' to the nations, by word (2:9) and also by deed (2:10-11).

4 *Coming*[14] *to him, that living stone,*
*rejected by men but in God's sight chosen and precious,*
5 *like living stones, you are yourselves being built into a spiritual house,*
*to be a holy priesthood, to offer spiritual sacrifices*
*acceptable to God through Jesus Christ.*
6 *For it stands in scripture:*
*"Behold, I am laying in Zion a stone,*
*a cornerstone chosen and precious,*
*and he who believes in him will not be put to shame."*
7 *To you therefore who believe, he is precious,*
*but for those who do not believe,*
*"The very stone which the builders rejected*
*has become the head of the corner,"*
8 *and*
*"A stone that will make men stumble, a rock that will make them fall";*

---

14. Peter's Greek could support the imperative 'come' (as RSV) but equally the participle 'coming'; the latter is preferred because of the flow of the sentence. Once again (as in 1:18), we have a verb that connects with the previous words, without full stop: 'For you have tasted that the Lord is kind, *coming* to him...you are yourselves being built...'.

*for they stumble because they disobey the word, as they were*
*destined to do.*
9 *But you are* *a chosen race,*
*a royal priesthood,*
*a holy nation,*
*God's own people,*
*that you may declare the wonderful deeds of him*
*who called you out of darkness into his marvellous light.*
10 *Once you were no people but now you are God's people;*
*once you had not received mercy but now you have received mercy.*

It is important to tease apart the cluster of ideas in this passage.

(i) The central teaching here is that Jesus Christ the Lord is the 'stone' (verse erses 4, 6, 7, 8) prophesied in the Old Testament (Psalm 118:22; Isaiah 8:14; 28:16). From these texts (and Peter's comments on them) we learn that God values Christ as 'precious' whereas men typically reject him.

Peter is reflecting upon the impact of the Gospel-word on these people of northern Anatolia. The readers of his letter have 'come' to Christ and 'believed' in him. Accordingly, they will not be 'put to shame' (verse 6 quoting Isaiah 28:16), that is, not found wanting on the Last Day. Furthermore, Christ will be for them and fellow-believers the 'corner stone' that will support them as 'living stones' in God's heavenly temple.

On the other hand, there are many local people (including, perhaps, former friends of the readers) who have rejected Christ. They too have heard the Gospel-word and upon examining this 'stone', found him unworthy of their confidence, just as the chief priests in Jerusalem had previously done with Jesus (Mark 12:10). This is a frightening picture. It is almost beyond imagination to contemplate someone looking at Christ from every side, like a masonry stone as it were, and then saying, 'I reject him' and casting him aside.

As in all things in life, there are consequences that follow the choices we make. Do those who choose to reject Christ think there will be no consequences? For them, says Peter, Christ is 'a stone of stumbling and a rock of offence' (verse 8 citing Isaiah 8:14). On the Day of Judgment, believers in

Christ will 'not be put to shame' whereas disbelievers will 'stumble' over him to their destruction.

We cannot help noticing that just as Christ is 'chosen by God' but 'rejected by men' (2:4), so too Christians are 'chosen...by God' but, like their Master, are rejected and 'reviled' as wrongdoers (1:1; 2:11; 3:16). There is a commonality of divine election and human rejection that is true of Christ and his people. Furthermore, Christ's noble behaviour under humanity's abusive rejection is the living example his disciples are to follow (2:21).

(ii) God is 'building' a 'spiritual house' on Christ the 'cornerstone' (verses 6, 7). He is the 'living stone', who (a) is alive through his resurrection (1:3), and (b) gives 'life' to those who 'come' to him.

Peter has understood well his Lord's teaching about the temple. Jesus prophesied the destruction of that great structure in Jerusalem. It was one of the most imposing buildings in the world. Jews saw it as the great sign that they were God's special people. While it stood not even Roman occupation could shake their faith in their divine election. Jesus, however, said he would replace it with his heavenly 'church' (Matthew 16:18). Accordingly, the apostolic writers like Peter and Paul regularly refer to the local gathering of believers as God's temple, indwelt by his Spirit (see for example 1 Corinthians 3:16).

(iii) Having introduced his teaching about the 'spiritual house' Peter moves on immediately to a more central idea, that is, the gathered people as a 'holy priesthood' (verse 5). Soon he will also call them a 'royal priesthood' (verse 9).

As a 'holy' and 'royal' 'priesthood' they have one major function, 'to offer spiritual sacrifices'. Under the Old Testament the High Priest offered animal sacrifices to God. These, however, only anticipated the sacrifice to end all sacrifices. Once Jesus had offered himself 'once and for all' as the sacrifice for sins all other sacrifices were superseded, ended (see Hebrews 10:3-14).

New Testament writers often use the vocabulary of sacrifice in a metaphorical way.

> Through [Christ]
> let us continually offer up a sacrifice of praise to God,
> that is, *the fruit of lips* that acknowledge his name
> (Hebrews 13:15).

> ...present *your bodies* as a living sacrifice,
> holy and acceptable to God
> (Romans 12:1).

> *Religion* that is *pure* and *undefiled* before God and the Father
> is this: to visit widows and orphans in their affliction,
> and to keep oneself unstained from the world.
> (James 1:27).

Likewise metaphorical is the 'holy priesthood' that 'offers spiritual sacrifices acceptable to God' (verse 5). Under the new covenant *the people* offer 'spiritual sacrifices' when they praise God for calling them 'out of darkness into his marvellous light'. How does God 'call' them? It is by his Gospel-word, focused on Christ. Their 'darkness' was the 'futile way of life' inherited from their forebears (1:18), the passions of their former ignorance (1:14).

This 'praise' of God for his redemption has a rich background in the Psalms, for example:

> I have made the Lord God my refuge,
> that I may *tell* of all thy *works*.
> (Psalm 73:28).

> Then we thy people, the flock of thy pasture,
> will give thanks to thee forever;
> from generation to generation we will *recount* thy praise.
> (Psalm 79:13).

> Let them thank the Lord for his steadfast love,
> for his wonderful *works* to the sons of men!
> And let them offer sacrifices of thanksgiving,
> and *tell* of his *deeds* in songs of joy.
> (Psalm 107:21-22).

The people of Israel could never forget their deliverance from Egypt nor the Lord's continuing shepherd-like care of them as a people and as individuals. Accordingly, with a deep sense of thankfulness they 'told' of his 'deeds' for them. Many Psalms were written as hymns of praise to God for his 'deeds' of salvation for the people.

Peter, then, expects that the people of the new Israel will likewise extol God's 'deeds', wrought through the death and resurrection of Jesus Christ delivering them from futility, divine judgment and death. They are now God's 'chosen race', his 'holy nation' and 'his own people' (Isaiah 43:20-21; Exodus 19:6).

Like original Israel, this 'new Israel' (which now includes Gentiles) were '*once* not a people...*once* not recipients of God's mercy' (cf. Hosea 1:9; 2:1), but who are '*now*' the people of God because they have '*now*' received his mercy (when the Gospel-word was preached to them). In short, by declaring 'the deeds of him who *called you out of*[15] darkness into his marvellous light' Peter means the *congregational* praising of God for his mighty acts of salvation.

The likely setting, then, of Peter's words 'declare the deeds' of God is congregational. But there are various other related meanings, for example, an individual's testimony in church (or to an outsider) or a church's evangelistic outreach. It would not be true to Peter's intention to limit the meaning of 'declare' to congregational 'telling forth' the saving works of Christ.

Two things are clear from verses 4-10. First, God has a positive purpose in choosing and saving his people. It is that they 'tell forth' God's mighty deeds for their redemption. Church people sometimes worry about the moral and philosophical problems associated with election since it implies the non-election of others. For his part, Peter states that God has chosen and redeemed his people so that they will be his light to the Gentiles, both by their words and deeds.

Second, it is clear that their 'telling forth' is to be heartfelt

15. See Hosea 11:1 'When Israel was a child, I loved him, and *out of* Egypt I *called* my son', meaning redemption out of slavery in Egypt.

and joyous and not merely a religious duty. Let the redeemed never forget the moral and spiritual prison from which they are now free. A thankful heart is a free heart and that is what God desires for us.

This 'telling forth' cannot be separated from the behaviour of the people of God in the wider society. To this we now turn.

*Reflection on verses 4-10:* We are reminded by the re-run of Israel's 'story' that God is by nature a rescuer of the lost and the spiritually imprisoned. God has re-birthed Father-less people who were without hope to be his children with a 'living hope'. In doing so God brings people into a family, which Peter calls 'a spiritual house'; it is not good for God's children to be alone and unattached. Jesus Christ is the foundation 'stone' of that 'house', though to those who reject him he is 'a stone of stumbling'. When that 'spiritual house' assembles its members are a 'holy priesthood' that joyfully and thankfully praises God for his wonderful deeds.

# 2

# God's People: In the World

## 1 Peter 2:11-3:8

Peter begins a new section of his letter with the words, 'Beloved, I beseech you...'. Even the casual reader notices the sequence that follows; where he addresses in turn the 'aliens and exiles' (2:11-17), 'servants' (2:18-25), 'wives' (3:1-6), 'husbands' (3:7) and finally, 'all of you' (3:8-12).

Peter is adapting a practice found in various Greek and Jewish writings of the times, which stated the 'duties' of various groups. There is a difference, however. Peter's instructions are filled with the teachings and example of Jesus.

We saw in the first part of the letter that believers are now thought of as the 're-born' and 'redeemed' people of God (1:3, 18), whose story re-traces the story of old Israel, though to a transcendent degree. Peter concluded that part of his letter by encouraging the people as a 'holy and 'royal' priesthood to 'offer spiritual sacrifices acceptable to God through Jesus Christ'. They were to declare 'the wonderful deeds of him who called [them] out of darkness into his marvellous light' (2:5, 9). This 'telling forth' will occur within the congregation as well as members of the congregation sharing the Gospel-word with unbelievers.

Peter is deeply aware, however, that the 'Gentiles' (2:12), that is, unbelievers, will be quick to criticise any moral failure or inconsistency by believers. This extended section, therefore, spells out the sort of behaviour that will silence criticisms. More than that, however, their Christ-like behaviour will 'flesh out' their verbal message and be an unspoken challenge to unbelievers.

## GOOD CONDUCT AMONG THE GENTILES (2:11-12)

2:11 *Beloved, I beseech you as aliens and exiles*
*to abstain from the passions of the flesh that wage war against your soul.*

2:12 *Maintain good conduct among the Gentiles,*
*so that in case they speak against you as wrongdoers,*
*they may see your good deeds and glorify God on the day of visitation.*

There are three parts to this short passage: (i) Peter's address to his readers; (ii) his appeal; (iii) his purpose in making his appeals.

(i) Verses 11 and 12 are almost a second beginning to the letter. In his opening words Peter addressed his readers as 'exiles of the Dispersion' (1:1). Here he calls them 'aliens and exiles' who are living 'among the Gentiles' (verse 12), that is, 'dispersed' across the world. As 'aliens' they are non-citizens where they currently live, 'exiles' from their homeland (heaven).

There is a parallel that illustrates Peter's description of believers. At that time there was a 'Diaspora' of Jews living outside Palestine among the Gentiles, who regarded the land of Israel as their one true home. In other words, Peter is telling Christian believers that they are the new, true Israel, God's Diaspora scattered among the nations, away from their true home in heaven.

During the next century a brief but interesting work called the *Epistle to Diognetus* appeared. It is not known who wrote it or to whom it was written, except that Diognetus appears to have been a person of high rank who wanted to learn more about Christianity. In the course of this Epistle the writer picks up several of Peter's ways of thinking about believers as 'dispersed' throughout the world (as indicated by the italics):

> ...while living in Greek and barbarian cities,
> according as each has obtained his lot,
> and following the local customs,

both in clothing and in food, and in the rest of life,
they *show forth* the wonderful and confessedly strange
character of the constitution of their own citizenship.
They dwell in their own fatherlands, but as if *sojourners* in them;
they share all things as citizens, and suffer all things as if
*strangers*.
Every foreign country is their fatherland,
and every fatherland is a foreign country....

The writer goes on to liken Christians in the world in the way the Greeks contrasted the 'soul' (eternal) with the 'body' (temporal).

...what the *soul* is in the body,
that the Christians are in the world.
The soul is *spread throughout* all members of the body,
and Christians throughout the cities of the world.
The soul dwells in the body, and Christians dwell in the world,
but are not of the world. (*Epistle to Diognetus* v1, vii [Loeb edition]).

This 'soul' and 'body' language is not something we find in the Bible. Nonetheless, the writer has grasped the idea of Christians as 'dispersed' throughout the world and who are, as its 'soul', the critical source of its wellbeing. This reminds us of Jesus describing his people as 'salt' that preserves the world from corruption and 'light' for its moral darkness (Matthew 5:13-14). A world without Christ's influence is a dark and dangerous place.

Jeremiah's letter from Jerusalem to the exiles in Babylon in the sixth century before Christ mentions *exiles* and *Babylon*, references that also appear in First Peter (1:1, 17; 2:11; 5:13).

1 These are the words of the letter which Jeremiah the prophet
sent from Jerusalem to the elders of the *exiles*, and to the
priests, the prophets, and all the people, whom Nebuchadnezzar
had taken into *exile* from Jerusalem to *Babylon*.
3 ... It said:
4 "Thus says the LORD of hosts, the God of Israel,
to all the *exiles* whom I have sent into *exile* from Jerusalem to
*Babylon*:

5 Build houses and live in them; plant gardens and eat their produce.
6 Take wives and have sons and daughters;
take wives for your sons, and give your daughters in marriage, that they may bear sons and daughters; multiply there, and do not decrease.
7 But seek the welfare of the city where I have sent you into *exile*, and pray to the LORD on its behalf, for in its welfare you will find your welfare.
(Jeremiah 29:1-7)

Remarkably, despite their 'exile' in Babylon Jeremiah calls for positive attitudes and actions towards the city where God's people are captives. He urges them, 'seek the welfare of the city and to pray to the LORD on its behalf'. Similar attitudes are implicit in Peter's words to these 'aliens and exiles' (2:13-17), despite their present sufferings that show signs of becoming even more intense.

(ii) Peter makes two appeals, one negative the other positive (verses 11b, 12a).

(a) He calls on them to 'abstain from fleshly lusts that war against the soul'. Peter is reminding them of their 'former' way of life when they were being 'conformed by...passions' (1:14), 'the futile ways inherited from [their] fathers' (1:18). This was before God 'called [them] out of darkness into his marvellous light' (2:9).

What does Peter mean? The answer is likely found in his demand, 'let the time that is past suffice for doing what the Gentiles like to do, living in licentiousness, passions, drunkenness, revels, carousing and lawless idolatry' (4:3). They had been totally self-centred, pursuing sensual pleasures through sexual promiscuity and drinking bouts, a life that expressed total denial of God.

Peter's description of these things as 'passions' (or cravings) is insightful, since they easily exercise a vice-like grip on those who have lived like this. He also understands that they 'war against the soul'. True, Peter is equally concerned that believers 'cast off' the social evils of malice, deceit, hypocrisy, envy and slander (2:1). While these are not easy to abandon, we should not underestimate the addictive powers of sexual practices, gambling, and alcohol and substance abuse.

'Fleshly lusts' promise much, but deliver only despair and bondage. Peter warns against returning to these bad old ways since they bring only inner conflict ('war against the soul'), spiritual confusion and deepening guilt.

Peter's negative injunction, while important, is made in passing (see 2:25). His greater concern here is the positive appeal' that he now makes.

(b) His appeal to 'have good conduct among the Gentiles' could be interpreted as a call for a polite morality and good manners. Educated classes were familiar with popular contemporary writings of, for example, Cicero, Seneca and Plutarch, who taught about self-control, bravery and other virtues.

By appealing for 'good conduct' is Peter merely endorsing popular notions of virtue and morality? This is to be doubted. The contemporary moralists' behaviour was based ultimately on self-centred living with the hopes of personal advancement. Peter's concern was for the glory of God (verse 12) through the imitation of Christ (as we shall see).

By 'good conduct' Peter was thinking of one's total way of life, in public or private, day and night, year by year. (The Greek term *anastrophē* is used throughout First Peter—1:15, 18; 3:1, 2, 16, cf. 1:17—and also by Paul in Galatians 1:13, Ephesians 4:22 and James 3:13.) By calling it 'good' Peter is using the aesthetic word 'beautiful' and has in mind a beautiful life, in its length and breadth. As we shall see, it is a beautiful manner of living because it imitates and is shaped by Jesus' life (and death).

These 'aliens and exiles' are Christian believers, God's new Israel living scattered among unbelievers, whom Peter calls 'Gentiles'. The 'good conduct' of these believers is for the sake of these Gentiles, as he now explains.

(iii) Peter's great concern is that believers 'glorify God' in the eyes of these 'Gentiles'. Peter refers to them as 'foolish men' who, in their 'ignorance', are 'speaking against' Christians as 'evildoers' and who 'revile [their] good behaviour of life in Christ' (see also 2:15 and 3:16).

Why should these Gentiles display such antipathy towards believers? Later in the letter Peter comments on the unbelievers' surprise that these 're-born' and 'redeemed' people do 'not now join with them in the same wild profligacy' so that they now 'abuse' them (4:4). Evidently, those who continued in their old lifestyle were offended by the changed lives of their former comrades.

Peter's observation is confirmed by Roman writers of those times. Tacitus, who became governor of Asia (one of the provinces mentioned in 1:1), said that Christians were 'loathed for their vices' and that they were guilty of 'hatred of the human race' (*Annals* 15.44). Suetonius declared that Christians were 'a new and wicked superstition' (*Nero* 16).

Their contemporaries probably viewed Christians as a breakaway Jewish sect that refused to recognise the Roman emperor, preferring instead a person they called 'Christos' (smeared one). They were easily misunderstood or became the victim of misinformation. Participating in the 'body and blood' of Christ made them appear cannibals, just as marriage between a 'brother' and a 'sister' brought them condemnation as being incestuous.

What are the 'good works' that will bring glory to God in the eyes of unbelievers 'on the day of visitation'? We hear echoes of Jesus' teaching: 'Let your light so shine before men, that they may see your good works and give glory to your Father who is in heaven' (Matthew 5:16). In Peter's hand these 'good works' are the attitudes and actions of godly submission in society, workplace and family, as Peter goes on to explain. By 'good works' Peter does not mean the 'good manners' or civic virtue so prized (in theory!) in the Graeco-Roman world.

Peter's 'day of visitation' resonates with the many end-time references in the letter (1:5, 7; 4:7, 13; 5:1, 4) and points to the Last Day. It most likely also refers to a special moment *within* history such as when Jesus came to Israel bringing salvation (Luke 19:44) or when the Gospel-word comes to people presenting the opportunity for re-birth (1:25).

For the people of Anatolia the 'day of visitation' is the time when they hear the word of God. Paul called this 'the day of salvation' (2 Corinthians 6:2). Peter's point is that believers' behaviour creates a context in which people will listen to God's word. He is not teaching that 'good deeds' *in themselves* convert unbelievers but they establish an environment for the Gospel-word to do so.

Peter explains what he means later in his comments about the wife who is married to an unbeliever. By her behaviour alone, without a word (the Gospel), she will 'win' the husband who has not yet obeyed that word (see 3:1-2). Peter is not teaching that spiritual re-birth is possible apart from the Gospel-word, for that would be to deny what he has already said (1:25). Rather, he is pointing to the potent effects of behaviour that is truly Christian. Godly behaviour matters and must not be separated from the word of God.

## GOOD CONDUCT AMONG THE GENTILES: SOCIETY (2:13-17)

The first item in Peter's 'house-table' is his 'appeal' (see 2:11) to the 'aliens and exiles' to 'be subject to every human institution', specifically the world kingdom ruled by the Roman emperor through his provincial governors.

Even a superficial reading of Peter's words brings to mind those of his fellow apostle Paul in his Letter to the Romans.

| 1 Peter 2 | | Romans 13 | |
|---|---|---|---|
| 13 | **Be subject**...to every human institution | 1 | Let every person **be subject** to the governing authorities. |
| 14 | governors...punish **those who do wrong** | 3-4 | rulers...execute [God's] wrath on **the wrongdoer** |
| 17 | **honour** the emperor | 7 | [Render] **honour** to whom honour is due. |

The similarity of language and ideas are striking and call for explanation. Perhaps Peter copied from Paul, or vice versa? That seems unlikely since we would have expected even more words in common. Most likely there was a body of teaching that came from the Lord Jesus that Paul and Peter in turn adapted to their respective situations, in their oral teaching and in their written instructions to the churches (see also 1 Timothy 2:1-2; Titus 3:1).

We recall from the Gospels that Jesus upheld a positive attitude to the state both by word and deed. To the test question about the lawfulness of paying tax to Rome he replied, 'render to Caesar the things that are Caesar's' (Mark 12:17). Despite Pontius Pilate's misuse of authority, Jesus submitted to the governor's authority as God-given (John 19:11).

Jesus stood in diametrical opposition to the 'zealot' policies of Judas the Galilean who in AD 6-7 took up the sword against the Romans over that very issue, the payment of tax by the godly to the ungodly. In a radical way Jesus and his apostles taught that believers must submit to and honour rulers, including those who are not believers. We must not underestimate the importance of this teaching since it commits Jesus' disciples to a positive and engaged attitude even to an ungodly society.[16]

A Roman governor acting on behalf of the Roman emperor killed Jesus. Yet within a brief time his apostles were teaching congregations to 'be subject' to those same officials. Did those apostles do a theological somersault? Did they weakly capitulate to the invincible might of Rome? By no means! They merely articulated their Master's own example and teaching.

Both Peter (in verses 13-17) and Paul (in Romans 13:1-7) apply the Lord's words and actions to believers in the 'city' where they live as 'aliens' and 'exiles', whether in Rome or in the towns and villages of Anatolia.

---

16. This changes where the ruler of the day makes himself a 'messiah', that is, an anti (or substitute) Christ. The negative attitude of the book of Revelation to the emperor (Domitian?) is due to that ruler's pretensions to be worshipped as a god.

13 *Be subject for the Lord's sake to every human institution,*
*whether it be to the emperor as supreme,*
14 *or to governors as sent by him to punish those who do wrong*
*and to praise those who do right.*
15 *For it is God's will that by doing right*
*you should put to silence the ignorance of foolish men.*
16 *Live as free men, yet without using your freedom as a pretext*
*for evil;*
*but live as servants of God.*
17 *Honor all men.*
*Love the brotherhood.*
*Fear God.*
*Honor the emperor.*

We make four observations from these verses.

(i) Peter's injunction to 'be subject' (verse 13) implies that civil obedience is first and foremost an attitude of heart and mind. Had it been a command to 'be obedient' it would likely have issued a slavish and passive resentment towards authority, rather than the positive outlook Peter's words imply.

Another reason that to 'be subject' is positive is inferred from the kind of people to whom believers were to 'be subject', that is, 'every human institution'. The RSV struggles to translate Peter's actual words that are (literally), 'every human creation'. By this he means those activities created by humanity for its good. Society is founded upon such 'human creations' (government, the work-place, family) and they give it stability. Consider the anarchy and breakdown of law and order where these institutions have become dysfunctional.

Specifically Peter means 'the emperor as supreme' and 'governors sent by him'. These were indeed 'human' and oppressive (Mark 10:42). Contemporary writers often describe them as corrupt, for example, Josephus portrays Emperor Tiberius likening provincial governors to blood-sucking flies (*Antiquities of the Jews* 18.172-176). Nonetheless, these authorities built cities with fine facilities for the people and established a network of roads throughout the empire. Not least, they maintained law and order, punishing wrongdoers and rewarding benefactors and others who did good works within society.

Furthermore, and of prime importance, Peter's appeal 'be subject' is 'for the Lord's sake', a teaching that has several connecting aspects. One is that Jesus is indeed 'Lord', whereas the 'human creations' are just that, *human*. The *Lord* Jesus is the One to be 'feared' rather than a fallible emperor (see 3:14-15). Moreover, since even this mighty Lord had been 'subject' to a lowly governor in recognition of his God-given authority (John 19:11). Being 'subject for the Lord's sake' means that his people are to follow his example (see also 2:21). Furthermore, such submission by his followers will tell the world what manner of Lord he is. In imitating the Lord's humility his people will bear witness to him which, though wordless, is nonetheless potent.

(ii) Peter's appeal to 'be subject to emperor...governors' (who punish wrongdoers) is to dispel the misinformation that believers are, indeed, wrongdoers (who need to be punished). We recall his injunction (2:12) that believers 'maintain good conduct' lest the 'Gentiles' (local unbelievers) 'speak against' them as 'wrongdoers'. By 'doing right' (verse 15) that is, being subject to authorities, believers will bear witness to the Lord Jesus and at the same time 'silence the ignorance of foolish men' (verse 15).

By 'ignorance' Peter means those who have 'no knowledge' of God. This 'ignorance' of God was previously the way of these believers (1:14 'your *former* ignorance') as it is the way of the 'Gentiles' among whom they live. Their 'ignorance' of God is expressed in the 'foolish' way of living that has 'no fear of God'. We remember that 'the fear of the Lord is the beginning of knowledge' and that 'fools despise wisdom and instruction' (Proverbs 1:7).

So 'foolish' are these 'ignorant' ones (then and now!) that disciples of the Lord need to be decisive in their attitudes and actions towards authorities.

(iii) Peter uses the paradox that believers are 'free', yet are also to be 'slaves' (verse 16),[17] a paradox also found in Paul's letters (Romans 6:22; 1 Corinthians 7:22; 9:19; Galatians 5:13).

The 'freedom' of the believer is in consequence of 'redemption' from the slavery to 'passions (cravings) of the former ignorance', 'futile ways inherited' from previous generations (1:14,18). This moral and spiritual liberation flows from the divine forgiveness based on the sin-bearing Christ (see 2:24).

Peter, however, is soberly aware that such 'freedom' can become a 'mask' behind which professed believers live inconsistent, even wicked lives. He insists, however, that this 'freedom' provides no opportunity for moral libertinism (which would merely mean a return to the passions of former ignorance). On the contrary, those who are now 'free' are to be the 'slaves of God', whose will they do without question.

*Reflection on verse 16:* God sets us free from sin to be his slaves. We must ask ourselves, 'Are we truly slaves of God or do we merely fit God into to a few convenient gaps we find for him?' Being God's slave means being conscious of his total ownership of us every day and trusting his fatherly love in every circumstance. It is not an onerous slavery, therefore, but one paradoxically in which we find our truest freedom.

(iv) Peter concludes this section (verse 17) with four strong and positive encouragements. The structure is interesting.

*17 Honor all men.*
*Love the brotherhood.*
*Fear God.*
*Honor the emperor.*

(a) The two *outer* injunctions exhort believers to 'honour' respectively 'all men' and 'the emperor'. Clearly, believers must respect and value outsiders.

---

17. Since the era of the King James Version translations have been coy about rendering the Greek *doulos* as 'slave', which indeed it truly is!

The two inner injunctions appeal to 'insiders' to 'love the brotherhood' and 'to fear God'. This inner core is prior to and the spiritual resource for the outer obligation to 'honour all' and to 'honour the emperor'.

(b) The two pairs of adjoining exhortations are likewise instructive. The first is global contrasting 'all men' in the empire with 'the (worldwide) brotherhood' of believers; the second is individual contrasting 'God' and 'the emperor'.

There are implicit challenges here. We are called to 'honour all men' but to 'love the brotherhood' takes priority. Likewise we 'honour' the emperor but more importantly we 'fear God'. Here Peter has adapted Jesus' famous words: 'Render to Caesar what is Caesar's (that is, honour); render to God what is God's (that is, fear)'.

*Reflection on verses 13-17:* Peter's words (like Paul's in Romans 13:1-7) have frequently been a source of painful tension. When subject to persecution it is difficult to honour the 'emperor' who is applying pressure to drive the believer from his faithfulness to God. Alternatively, it is hard to honour the 'emperor' who is demanding that Christians act against their conscience over, for example, conscription for military service. There is no doubt, however, where the right choice lies—we must always give priority to God over 'emperor' and to 'the brotherhood' over 'all men'.

## GOOD CONDUCT AMONG THE GENTILES: SLAVES (2:18-25)

Slavery has been all but eliminated in the developed world, though 'people trafficking' is still common in the developing world. In the New Testament era slavery was an everyday reality. It is likely that more people were slaves than free. Many of Peter's readers may have been slaves, that is, household slaves in the towns and cities since farm slaves from rural areas would not have been free to gather for church meetings. Doubtless these household slaves listened intently to these words.

Peter calls for a slave to submit to the 'master', who was

called the *paterfamilias* in that society. In the Graeco-Roman world the *paterfamilias* had absolute power over wife and children, and in effect over the slave. In this passage Peter speaks of the slave 'enduring pain', 'suffering unjustly' and 'being beaten'. There was little if anything the slave could do in those circumstances.

While some masters were 'kind and gentle' many were not. Peter speaks of those masters who were 'overbearing' (literally 'twisted' v18). Clearly the lot of a slave with a master like that was miserable, a life of torture and torment from which death was the only escape.

It is no surprise that Peter devotes so much of his letter to such a slave and, as we shall see, also to a wife of a *paterfamilias* (see 3:1-7). The unjust suffering of slaves and wives at the hands of these powerful men had much in common with the unjust sufferings of Jesus at the hands of Jewish and Roman authorities. The suffering slave and the suffering wife are powerful figures, who as they imitate Christ, 'portray' him to bystanders.

It is important, therefore, to understand what is really going on in this passage. On the surface it appears to be an item in a moral code setting out a slave's duty. A closer look, however, reveals that Peter's real intent is to urge the slave to engage in the mission of Christ, both to others and also for himself. In verses 18-23 Peter sets out the slave's mission to his master (and other slaves) and in verses 24-25 he urges repentance for the slave himself. These two aspects of ministry, objective and subjective, are signalled by repetition of the important purpose word 'that' (Greek: *hina* verses 21, 24).

Peter exhorts the suffering slave to silent witness to Christ in verses 18-23. As he suffers injustice patiently the slave 'imitates' Christ's sufferings. God gives his 'approval' to this 'patience' (verses 19-20) since the slave demonstrates his trust in God in his situation, as Christ demonstrated trust in his. Such word-less witness tells the master and other slaves about Christ and hopefully is a precursor to speaking the Gospel.

Peter shifts his focus to the slave's own repentance in verses 24-25. Once more the word 'that' is critical. Christ suffered for the slave's forgiveness *that* the slave (and all others) might 'depart from sin and live to righteousness' (verse 24).

In short, to regard verses 18-25 merely as an item in a moral code would be to miss its true intent, each signalled by the word 'that'. Peter points to the sufferings of Christ, on one hand, *that* the slave imitates them to 're-live' Christ to his master and other slaves, and on the other, *that* the slave himself will turn from his sins.

## SLAVES, BE SUBJECT TO YOUR MASTERS (2:18-20)

*2:18 Servants, be submissive to your masters with all respect,*
*not only to the kind and gentle but also to the overbearing.*
*2:19 For one is approved if, mindful of God, he endures pain while suffering unjustly.*
*2:20 For what credit is it,*
*if when you do wrong and are beaten for it you take it patiently?*
*But if when you do right and suffer for it you take it patiently,*
*you have God's approval.*

(i) On three counts Peter's appeal to slaves 'to be subject to masters' is surprising. First, slaves were not usually thought worth addressing, whereas Peter focuses more on them than any other group in this letter. Secondly, he does not point them to any task or duty as we might expect in a 'house-table', but merely enjoins patience. This is because he connects slavery under a cruel master with suffering, that is, *unjust* suffering. Thirdly, there is no corresponding appeal to masters, at least not explicitly. Implicitly, though, the master is encouraged to be 'kind and gentle' since these are the known qualities of the master of masters, Jesus (cf. Matthew 11:29-30).

(ii) Peter's appeal to slaves 'to be subject' to masters 'with all fear' (verse 18) is similar to his encouragement that a wife's behaviour be marked by 'fear' (3:2). The Greek word *phobos* means 'fear' in the sense of reverence for God and respect for man. But is Peter calling for a slave to 'fear' a twisted master and a wife to 'fear' a frightening[18] husband? These persons, indeed, were to be feared because of their capacity to harm the defenceless and vulnerable without limit or accountability. To the contrary, however, Peter is appealing to the slave and the wife to 'fear God' (2:17), just as he will appeal the persecuted believer to 'fear' Christ the Lord rather than the persecutor (see 3:14).

Because of that higher 'fear' (or reverence) to God and to Christ it will be possible for the slave to have a lesser 'fear' (or respect) for the earthly master and for the wife to 'fear' (or 'respect') her earthly husband. In other words, Peter is calling for a God-centred outlook (verse 19a). Literally: 'on account of conscience towards God' where 'conscience' does not imply feelings of guilt or innocence, but awareness of God's will and character.

(iii) The heart of the passage, then, is Peter's call for 'patience' for the slave who is suffering unjustly.

Here Peter structures his text powerfully (verses 19-20):

*For one is approved if,*
*mindful of God, he endures pain while suffering unjustly.*
*For what credit is it,*
*if when you do wrong and are beaten*[19] *for it*
*you take it patiently?*
*But if when you do right and suffer for it*
*you take it patiently,*
*you have God's approval.*

Peter's words are carefully formulated. They also adapt Jesus' words (where the word *charis*, translated 'credit') are

---

18. Peter's 'let nothing terrify you' (3:6) implies a 'frightening' life for this wife.
19. Peter's word 'beaten' (kolaphizomenoi) is rare in the NT, but it appears in Matthew's account of the members of the Sanhedrin beating Christ at his trial (Matt 26:67) and Mark's account of Roman soldiers beating Christ before the crucifixion (Mark 14:65). Peter's application of this word to cruelly treated slaves seems deliberate; Christ and such slaves had much in common.

used: 'If you love those who love you, what *credit* is that to you? For even sinners love those who love them. And if you do good to those who do good to you, what *credit* is that to you? For even sinners do the same. And if you lend to those from whom you hope to receive, what *credit* is that to you?'(Luke 6:32-34)

The passage begins and ends with the notion of God's 'approval' and the words 'you take it patiently' are repeated. Quite clearly, patience under unjust suffering has divine approval. Most likely this is because such 'patience' re-lives the way Christ bore his unjust sufferings at the hands of Pontius Pilate, as he will now say.

## CHRIST THE EXEMPLAR (2:21-23)

*2:21* *For to this you have been called,*
*because Christ also suffered for you,*
*leaving you an example, that you should follow in his steps.*
*2:22* *He committed no sin; no guile was found on his lips.*
*2:23* *When he was reviled, he did not revile in return;*
*when he suffered, he did not threaten;*
*but he trusted to him who judges justly.*

(i) It now becomes clear (verse 21) that the unjustly suffering slave has been 'called' to follow the example of Christ's unjust sufferings. In other words, Peter sees a special connection between Christ and the slave, just as he will see that connection between the suffering wife and Christ (3:1-6).

Indeed, Peter says it was for that very reason Christ 'suffered for you', that is, to leave behind an enduring example for the mistreated slave to follow.

Peter uses two powerful images to portray Christ as the exemplar for the suffering slave. He calls the patient Christ an 'example', a word then used for a child's writing stencil (or today a dressmaker's pattern). And he enjoins that slaves 'follow closely in his footsteps', in the manner of a disciple walking closely behind a rabbi. These are very different images, but they combine to provide a powerful impetus and consolation for the unjustly suffering slave.

(ii) Peter, witness to the sufferings of Christ (5:1), spells out what he means (verses 22-23):

Christ committed no sin; no guile was found on his lips;
who when reviled, did not revile in return;
who when suffering did not threaten;
but who handed himself over to him who judges justly.

Through Peter's words we see the silhouette of Christ on trial before the Sanhedrin and the Roman governor. He was innocent of the crime of treason for which he was charged. The crucifixion of Christ is the classic example of unjust punishment.

At the same time Jesus' *patient* behaviour is the paradigm for the unjustly punished slave, and beyond that to all people who are treated unjustly. Here we see Christ as a God-centred man, not at all as a man-centred man— a man of faith who 'handed over' his 'case' for the just judge's verdict on the last day.

The contrast with prevailing attitudes is stark. Typical was the attitude of the Greek writer Aeschylus: 'For word of hate let word of hate be said...and for murderous stroke let murderous stroke be paid' (*Choephori* 301, Loeb edition). It was the same in the Jewish world where, as the Maccabean martyrs died, they pleaded with God to punish their tormentors. Few things have changed the world's values in the way Jesus' patience under unjust suffering has done. Formerly Paul had been a violent zealot but as a man 'in Christ' he wrote, 'Never avenge yourselves...' (Romans 12:19). Many now think this way, thanks to the influence of Christ over two millennia.

## CHRIST THE SIN-BEARER (2:24-25)

*2:24 He himself bore our sins in his body on the tree,*
*that we might die to sin and live to righteousness.*
*By his wounds you have been healed.*
*2:25 For you were straying like sheep,*
*but have now returned to the Shepherd and Guardian of your souls.*

Here Peter expands upon Christ's sufferings, as to (i) their effects (sin-bearing), (ii) their purpose (departure from sins), and (iii) their consequences (turning to the shepherd).

(i) In verse 24a Peter picks up his earlier words in verse 21 that 'Christ also suffered for you'. Christ's suffering 'for' slaves was to show them what to do when they were treated unjustly, that is, behave patiently. Here, though, Christ sufferings are being described as atoning for sins.

> Christ also suffered for you...
> who himself bore our sins in his body on the tree...

Almost every word calls for comment.

(a) Since 'Christ *also* suffered' adds nothing to the meaning it is probably better translated as '*Even* Christ suffered'. In other words, Peter is astonished that the exalted Christ should suffer for a lowly person like a slave. Jews were looking for a victorious Christ, not a suffering Christ. Great was their astonishment and sense of offence at the very idea of 'Christ *crucified'* (see 1 Corinthians 1:22).

(b) 'Suffered' and 'suffering' are disproportionately prominent in this short letter and they portray Christ through the eyes of one who was a 'witness' to those sufferings (5:1). Paul's 'Christ died for' his people is less emotionally powerful than Peter's 'Christ *suffered* for you' (slaves and others).

(c) Peter's '...who himself bore our sins in his body' expands upon 'Christ...suffered *for* you'. The keyword is 'for' (Greek: *hyper*) which means that Christ suffered 'for the sake of' and 'in place of' others. Here is the bloodied Christ bearing the burden of the sins of others in his own body. It is a classic statement of Christ's atonement that has many parallels in the New Testament (see for example, Mark 10:45; 2 Corinthians 5:21; Hebrews 10:10; 1 John 2:2).

In this passage, more than any other in the New

Testament, Peter applies Isaiah's Fourth Servant Song to Jesus:

| | | |
|---|---|---|
| v22 | 'He committed no sin, no guile was found on his lips' | Isa 53:9 |
| v24a | 'He himself bore our sins' | Isa 53:4 |
| v24c | 'By his wounds you have been healed' | Isa 53:5 |
| v25 | You were 'like sheep going astray' | Isa 53:6 |

The centrality of Isaiah 53 in Peter's thinking is clear evidence that he saw Jesus' sufferings as a sacrifice for the sins of others in fulfilment of the Suffering Servant of the LORD.

(d) Peter's reference to 'on the tree' is one of many in the New Testament to Deuteronomy 21:23, which states that 'a hanged man is accursed by God'. Greater than Christ's physical sufferings, was his abandonment by God, enveloped in the sins of others. Here is the deepest of mysteries about God, that is, that human sin is atoned for substitutionally in the abandoned, 'accursed' person of the crucified Messiah.

(ii) In verse 24b Peter states the *purpose* of Christ's sufferings. Note that Peter has exchanged the pronoun 'you' (slaves) for 'we' (all believers). Christ suffered *for us in order that* they 'depart[20] from sins and live for righteousness'.

As recent converts ('newborn babes' 2:1) their memory of sins would have been pretty fresh. Christ's death has brought them freedom from their former dark moral and spiritual prison (1:14, 18). Let them, or us, not go back to that 'Egypt'! Rather, let those who are forgiven 'live for righteousness', that is, in their 'good manner of life in Christ' (3:16), including as responsible citizens within the wider community.

As so often in the letter (and the New Testament letters generally) we see the close connection between God's saving work for believers *and* the necessity for their expression of that salvation *ethically* (see also 1:22; 2:1; 2:11ff).

---

20. RSV has 'die to sins' perhaps to balance 'live to righteousness'.

(iii) Finally Peter gives the consequence of Christ's sufferings. He uses two unconnected images, one *medical* and the other *pastoral* (verses 24c-25):

> you were healed
> you have turned to the shepherd

Formerly these believers were *ignorant* of God (1:14), *trapped* in a moral prison (1:18), *diseased* and *lost*. Christ's vicarious death and his resurrection, as expressed in the Gospel-word, have brought them living hope, redemption and re-birth, and the healing and protection of the shepherd.

Most likely Peter wants us to understand that the 'healing' of which he speaks as being 'found by and cared for' by Christ the shepherd and overseer of souls. That 'healing' came at great cost, the terrible marks in the body of Christ sustained under flogging and crucifixion.

Christ portrays himself as the shepherd of the lost sheep in Israel in many places (Matthew 10:6; 15:24; Mark 6:34; 14:27-28; Luke 12:32; 15:3-7; 19:9-10; John 10:11). He powerfully fulfils Old Testament promises like Jeremiah 23:1-6 and Ezekiel 34:23 of a new David (Messiah) who will rescue and care for God's people. Peter, who was himself a shepherd of the Lord's people, is deeply conscious that the risen and ascended Christ is the 'chief shepherd' (5:4; cf. Hebrews 13:20 'the great shepherd of the sheep').

Just as old Israel knew that Yahweh was their shepherd, so too the aliens and exiles of the new Israel scattered across the world need to know that the Lord Jesus Christ is their shepherd. That will be true for all believers, but none more so than the desperately vulnerable slaves of cruel masters.

*Reflection on verses 18-25:* In recent times some people in developed societies have been able to take their cases of unjust sufferings to the courts. Yet even in such societies a mere fraction of wrongs are—or ever can be—righted. In developing countries the pursuit of justice is even more precarious. Most people who are wronged have no recourse to a sympathetic and fair hearing. The natural reaction is to seek payback and many wait their opportunity to strike back. That is not the way of Jesus either in life or in death. 'Forgive them', is his word to those suffering unjustly. That is true even where due process in the courts is possible and appropriate. Seeking justice (which may be appropriate) must be distinguished from seeking vengeance (which is forbidden).

Jesus' teaching and example support earthly rule as 'given' from God, even when that rule is imperfect. Some rule is usually better than anarchy.

Forgiveness (and, if possible, reconciliation) is God's gift to families, tribes, societies and nations. Without forgiveness the cycle of violence is never ending. Following Jesus' example breaks that cycle and allows families and communities to work together positively and constructively.

Patience and non-vindictive behaviour is not merely a moral virtue to aspire to; it flows out of a life that treads in the steps of Jesus. Equally, the 'grace' of forgiveness issues from one who knows that Jesus has borne sins in his own body, bringing healing of soul and the sense of belonging to the shepherd of souls.

That said, however, it is incumbent on a third party to seek the vindication of someone who has suffered unjustly. A person cannot stand by knowing, for example, that the reputation of an innocent person has been wrongly blemished or that someone has been wrongly imprisoned. In that situation a person must become an active advocate seeking justice for the wronged person.

Paul's instruction to Philemon about his runaway slave Onesimus is important. In that society slaves were typically regarded as unimportant. Paul, however, tells Philemon that the now-converted Onesimus is to be received back as a 'beloved brother' (Philemon 16-17). By late antiquity the impact of the Gospel, where all men were treated as equals before God, gradually diminished the phenomenon of slavery in Europe. The advent of European colonisation a thousand years later, however, witnessed once more the rise of the slave trade (from Africa) for the plantations in the New World. The eventual abolition of slavery was achieved in the main by the efforts of British evangelicals and President Abraham Lincoln in the United States. Regrettably, slavery is still a present reality in some developing countries.

## GOOD CONDUCT AMONG THE GENTILES: MARRIAGE (3:1-7)

This section of Peter's 'house-table' is unusual on two counts. First, in the two earlier sections he addressed only one side of the social relationship—citizens (but not rulers) and slaves (but not owners). Here he instructs wives *and* husbands. This may reflect the reality that many wives and husbands were believers, while few society leaders or slave owners were. As well, it signals Peter's view of the priority of family life, an attitude he had learned from Jesus (Mark 10:1-16).

Furthermore, for both spouses Peter's instructions have long-range *spiritual* intentions. Wives are to be subject to unbelieving husbands *in order* to win them in obedience to the Gospel-word and husbands are to care for their wives *in order* that prayers are not hindered. Godly home life is Peter's primary goal.

## WIVES, BE SUBJECT TO YOUR HUSBANDS (3:1-6)

1 *Likewise you wives, be submissive to your husbands,*
*so that some, though they do not obey the word,*
*may be won without a word by the behaviour of their wives,*
2 *when they see your reverent and chaste behaviour.*
3 *Let not yours be the outward adorning with braiding of hair,*
*decoration of gold, and wearing of fine clothing,*
4 *but let it be the hidden person of the heart*
*with the imperishable jewel of a gentle and quiet spirit,*
*which in God's sight is very precious.*
5 *So once the holy women who hoped in God*
*used to adorn themselves and were submissive to their husbands,*
6 *as Sarah obeyed Abraham, calling him lord.*
*And you are now her children if you do right and let nothing terrify you.*

Peter's instruction to wives follows a logical sequence, in three equal parts: (i) his injunction 'be subject' so as to win unbelieving husbands by 'behaviour' (verses 1-2); (ii) he explains that 'behaviour' (verses 3-4); (iii) he gives examples of the 'behaviour' of the 'holy women' (verses 5-6).

(i) Peter tells believing 'wives be subject to your[21] husbands' with the explicit intention of winning them for obedience to the word.

This is a most unusual statement since a wife was expected to adopt the beliefs of her husband, the all-powerful *paterfamilias*. According to Peter's near contemporary, the Gentile Plutarch (AD 46-120):

> It is becoming for the wife to worship and know only the gods that her husband believes in. (*Advice to Bride and Groom* 19; Loeb edition).

Conversion for the Jewish wife was, if anything, more difficult. According to Josephus (AD 37- *ca*. 95):

> The woman, says the Law, is in all things inferior to the man. Let her accordingly be submissive, not for humiliation, but that she may be directed; for God gave authority to the man. (*Against Apion* 2.201; Loeb edition).

Whether this woman is Gentile or Jew it has been a huge step for her to become a follower of Jesus. Equally huge is Peter's expectation that she will seek the conversion of a husband. Yet that is precisely his assumption and reveals the degree to which believers were expected to be mission-minded.

Peter engages in a word play when he writes, 'husbands...who do not obey the *word* may be won without a *word*' (verse 1). This means *both* the Gospel-word *and* the word-less behaviour that will 'win' the unbelieving husband. It would be a mistake to infer that Peter thinks conversion can occur without the Gospel-word. He has already taught us that we are redeemed by the blood of Christ (1:18) and 're-born' through the Gospel (1:23-25). Rather, he is saying

---

21. RSV omits 'your *own* husbands'. NT routinely specifies 'own' husbands to ensure that wives are not called upon to be subject to other husbands, or to men in general.

that the context and precursor to the husband's eventual conversion through the word will be his wife's behaviour.

(ii) What is the behaviour that will 'win' this unbeliever? There is ample evidence from the era that a woman might be tempted to think 'braiding of hair, decoration of gold, and wearing of fine clothing' (verse 3) would lead her husband to Christ. Peter is saying, he will not be won by her 'outward adorning' of herself or any other 'cosmetic' approach. It will be a quality *within* her expressed as a 'gentle and quiet spirit' (verse 4). Jesus said he was 'gentle and lowly in heart' (Matthew 11:29), using language very similar to Peter's. In short, Peter is calling on these wives to be 'Christ-like' *in heart*.

This inner quality, says Peter, is imperishable[22], unlike hair styling, jewellery or clothing which 'perish' or go out of fashion soon enough. In God's sight, says Peter, this 'gentle and quiet spirit' is 'very precious' (verse 4). Here Peter is reversing human values which prize physical beauty and outward adornment.

(iii) Peter gives examples of this inner beauty. He points to the inner adornment of 'holy women who hoped in God', that is to say, the wives of the Patriarchs (particularly Sarah) who 'were submissive to their husbands' (verse 5).

By way of example, he refers to Sarah who 'obeyed Abraham, calling him Lord' (verse 6). This is possibly misleading since in the presenting text (Genesis 18:12) the aged Sarah says, 'After my Lord is old, will I have this pleasure [of childbearing]?' Here Sarah does not *address* Abraham as 'Lord' (though she would have done so as a convention of those times) nor does she obey him (though she did on other occasions[23]).

---

22. 'Imperishable' occurs elsewhere in First Peter (1:4, 23) and points to the secure and eternal values rather than insecure and transitory ones. RSV's 'jewel' is not in Peter's original text.
23. In Genesis 12:5 'Abraham *took* Sarah...'; in 18:6 he directs her to bake; in 12:13 and 20:13 he encourages her to do as he desires. By contrast, in 16:2 Sarah encourages Abraham to do as she desires and in 21:12 God commands Abraham to do as Sarah desires. There were two sides to their relationship!

Peter points to these holy women and Sarah because of their hope in God's promises, expressed in their submissive attitudes to their husbands, which is reflected in their obedience to them.

One principle of biblical interpretation is to treat the biblical injunction as primary and the supporting Old Testament example as just that, a *supporting example*. Genesis 18:12 is illustrative, an example and not a direct command. Peter's primary appeal is for wives to 'be subject'; reference to 'holy women' and so Sarah's action is secondary, an example.

The Christian wife is first and foremost to 'be subject' to her husband arising from her 'hope in God' like the 'holy women' of earlier times. He is not telling a wife to call a husband 'Lord', nor is he instructing her to obey his commands (which may lead only to a sullen attitude).

*Reflection on verses 1-6:* Winning a husband for obedience to the Gospel was a priority for a wife in the New Testament era (see also 1 Corinthians 7:16). Yet she is not to preach at him, or attempt to entice him by self-adornment, but rather to win him by inner submission arising from Christ-like attitudes ('reverent and chaste...gentle and quiet spirit...hope in God'). Peter is not encouraging women to be dowdy but discouraging a 'cosmetic' approach to soul winning!

Peter's words for a wife to 'be subject to her husband' sound rather harsh to our ears today. In this regard (as noted from verse 6 above), we note that Peter does not call on a wife to 'obey' a husband. Clearly she is encouraged (a) to continue as a believer regardless of his outlook, and (b) to convert him.

It appears, then, that for a wife to 'be subject' really means 'to honour' her husband. Her attitude is analogous in some ways to the member of society whose 'subjection to' the emperor is expressed in 'honouring' the emperor (2:13, 17). Of course, the relationship of wife to husband is deeper than that of a citizen to the emperor. Wife and husband are one flesh and united to each other until 'death do them part' (see Mark 10:1-10).

It would be a mistake to imagine that women were entirely silent and passive at that time. That is not a true picture of either Jewish or Gentile households. We recall the portrayal of the ideal woman found in Proverbs 31:10-31 who is busy and proactive in managing her household. Likewise the Gentile wife was responsible for the conduct of domestic affairs within the household, including the control of the family budget and the supervision of household slaves. True, the man was a household's public face to the wider world, yet wives were anything but passive and silent and ruled as queens at home.

Nonetheless, many will regard this teaching as outmoded and unhelpful. It should be noted, however, that both the Pauline and Petrine texts call on wives to 'be subject' to husbands (see Ephesians 5:22; Colossians 3:18; 1 Timothy 2:11; Titus 2:4), so their combined teachings should not be put aside lightly. Furthermore, such texts are quite brief and give no detail as to how they are to be implemented. The most fundamental idea is that husbands have a God-given role and responsibility toward wives (see verse 7) that wives are to understand and appreciate. While every couple will work this out in their own way, we should understand that Peter's teaching expresses an overriding principle of Christian living that transcends culture and historical setting.

## HUSBANDS (3:7)

In addressing husbands Peter completes the corresponding side of this part of the 'house-table'.

In his injunction to husbands we see several words and ideas in verse 7 that are in common with Paul's directives to the men of Thessalonica (based here on literal translation of the Greek).

| 1 Peter 3:7 | 1 Thessalonians 4:4 |
| --- | --- |
| live together according to **knowledge** | that each one of you **know** |
| bestowing **honour** on the woman | how to take a **vessel** for himself |
| as the weaker **vessel** | in holiness and **honour** |

The items in common mean either that one author has depended on the other or, more probably, that Paul and Peter are adapting an earlier instruction that had been formulated in the years following Jesus' ministry. This indicates how seriously the apostles regarded married life especially in contrast with the freewheeling sexuality of that era.

*Likewise you husbands,*
*live considerately [with your wives]*     *as the weaker sex,*
*bestowing honour on the woman*     *as a joint heir of the grace of life*
*in order that your prayers may not be hindered.*

The passage is rather symmetrical in structure with two imperatives, each followed by 'as'. (I have departed from RSV in order to bring out the balanced nature of Peter's text; the word 'wives' does not occur in the original.) Thus it falls into three parts: (i) address to husbands; (ii) two imperatives regarding wives (live considerately; bestow honour), each of which qualifies a wife (*as* the weaker sex; *as* a joint heir of grace); (iii) the purpose of the imperatives (sustained common prayer).

(i) The initial 'Likewise' serves as a marker to begin addressing husbands. Some have argued that 'likewise' demands an exact and symmetrical reciprocity, but it is unlikely that husbands are to 'be subject' to their wives. Rather, the 'likewise' signals the next item to be addressed (see also 3:1; 5:5).

(ii) The Christian husband cannot in any way be like the Roman *Paterfamilias* or, for that matter, the rather patriarchal Jewish husband. The two imperatives teach that the Christian husband is not free to do as he chooses with his wife.

First, he is to 'live with' her 'considerately', or more precisely, 'according to knowledge', that is, with an informed understanding of her constitution. In turn, this implies gentleness towards her 'as the weaker vessel'. Most likely Peter is addressing the husband's sexual expectations and behaviour towards her, including during times of pregnancy and following childbirth.

Secondly, Peter enjoins the husband to 'bestow honour' on the woman, that is, to respect and look up to her. This is because she, with him, is a 'joint heir of the grace of life'. There are no sexual distinctions in heaven; both men and women share equally in their 'imperishable inheritance' that is 'kept in heaven' for them (1:3-4).

Thirdly, this implies his sexual fidelity to her. In that 'man's world' men had courtesans for their intellectual and sexual pleasure, concubines for their daily sexual indulgence and wives to provide heirs and run the home! In Christian marriage, a wife is to be *everything* and to mean *everything* to their husband.

(iii) The purpose of the two imperatives is so that their common prayers together are not hindered. We recall also 1 Corinthians 7:5 where household prayer is also envisaged. It is striking, therefore, that passing references in both Paul and Peter point to prayer together as fundamental part of Christian marriage.

Most likely this was without cultural precedent, whether in the Jewish or the Gentile cultures, and owes its origin to the brief period between Jesus and the earliest New Testament writings, stemming ultimately from Jesus himself.

*Reflection on verse 7:* The woman is 'weaker' than the husband (although in many ways women have greater physical endurance), yet he is to 'honour' her. This is unusual because elsewhere 'honour' is mostly directed to those who hold high office. Here honour is directed to the weaker. Accordingly, these imperatives are diametrically opposed to ideas of male patriarchy or masculine machismo, whether ancient or modern, where women are treated as inferior.

Just as wives are to be subject to husbands for a spiritual intent (the winning of their husbands), husbands are to be considerate towards and honour wives for a spiritual intent (their shared prayer life). These spiritual intentions are above and beyond their differing responsibilities towards each other and make a marriage the basic and most fundamental 'church', a place of prayer, godly nurture and care.

Earlier we noted the influence of Jesus' teaching and example regarding (pagan) political authority issuing in respect and cooperation with civil authorities (see 2:13-17). To that must be added the apostolic teaching about marriage life, its unity, mutual respect and shared prayer life.

## GOOD CONDUCT AMONG THE GENTILES: CHRIST-LIKENESS (3:8)

The opening word 'finally' signals that this passage concludes Peter's instructions to the 'aliens' and 'exiles' about their 'good behaviour' towards the 'Gentiles' among whom they are 'scattered' (see 2:11-12).

His address to 'all of you' is directed to the world-wide 'brotherhood' (2:17; 5:9), in particular to believers in the provinces of Pontus, Galatia, Cappadocia, Asia and Bithynia.

This passage bears a close relationship with Romans 12.

| | 1 Peter 3 | | Romans 12 |
|---|---|---|---|
| v8 | have **one mind** | v16 | **think** the **same** things |
| | **brotherly love** | v10 | **brotherly love** |
| | **humble** minded | v16 | the **humble** |
| v9 | not **returning evil for evil** | v17 | [not] **rendering evil for evil** |
| | on the contrary, **bless** | v14 | **bless** those who persecute you |

Has one writer been depending on the other, or more likely, are both Paul and Peter adapting an earlier, pre-formed apostolic tradition? Again, we make the point that these teachings flow from the wellspring of Jesus' teachings and life.

*3:8* *Finally, all of you have*
*unity of spirit,*
*sympathy,*
*love of the brethren,*
*a tender heart and*
*a humble mind.*

The five items Peter mentions in verse 8 are each matters of *attitude* to one another in the family of believers. The list begins and ends with words to do with the mind – 'one mind' and 'a humble mind'. In between are words that sound more emotive: 'sympathy' (literally, fellow-suffering), 'love of brothers and sisters' (see also 1:22) and 'tender heart' (better, 'compassion').

Several words in this list remind us of Jesus. He declared himself to be 'lowly of heart' (Matthew 11:29) and those present with him noticed his compassion to those in need (cf. Mark 1:41).

It may be no accident that Peter speaks of *five* positive attitudes to adopt and express. Earlier he spoke of five evils for the re-born to 'cast off', that is, malice, guile, insincerity, envy and slander (2:1). Peter may be making the point that authentic Christian living has both negative (things to cast off) and positive aspects (things to do).

Peter's readers were living with uncertainty and a likely worsening situation in relation to wider society. Peter has already hinted at this (1:6-7; 2:12, 15) and every indication points to troubled times ahead (3:13-4:6; 4:12-19; 5:6-10). Peter is saying, 'Do not let these difficult times bring out the worst in you, but the qualities of Jesus Christ.'

*Reflection on verse 8:* When times are bad, as they were becoming for Peter's readers, we easily become self-centred, forgetting to love one another. Under the persecutions of the coming centuries Christians often became judgmental and unloving towards one another. The injunctions in verse 8 to unity, sympathy, love, compassion and humility will always be appropriate, but never more so than in times of stress and difficulty.

## CONCLUSION: GOD'S PEOPLE IN THE WORLD (2:11-3:8)

'Maintain good conduct among the Gentiles' said Peter at the beginning of this section of the letter (2:11). In the 'house-table' that followed Peter has instructed citizens, slaves, wives and husbands, and all believers as to the nature of that 'good conduct'.

His teaching, however, has not been a list of moral duties as in the contemporary 'house-tables'. Peter's instruction about God and emperors encapsulates his view of the world as God-centred and not man-centred. Believers are to 'fear' God and they are only to 'honour' the emperor. Emperors, governors, slave masters and husbands only have a lesser authority; absolute authority is found only in God. For this reason believers are to be subject to human institutions – citizens to Roman government, slaves to masters, wives to husbands – knowing that they are just that, *human* institutions that are themselves subject to the majesty of God.

Like the Hebrew captives exiled in Babylon who were to 'seek the welfare' of that city we sense that Peter is urging a similar positive approach to this 'new' Israel exiled among the Gentiles whose capital is 'Babylon' (= Rome). His repeated injunction to 'be subject' implies voluntary, active and cooperative acceptance of human authority that itself is under the mighty hand of God (cf. 5:6).

This 'good conduct among the Gentiles' is not an end in itself, but is 'to glorify God on the day of visitation' (2:12). The unjustly suffering slave's imitation of Christ has a missionary intent, that is, to proclaim Christ (without words) to the master and other slaves. The wife's word-less 'good conduct' is to win her husband to the Lord. The husband's care of his wife is to enhance their prayer life together. In other words, the believer's 'good deeds', while good in themselves, have an underlying and ultimate missionary intent, to support the effectiveness of the Gospel-word when God 'visits' those unbelievers.

# 3

# Who Will Harm You?

## 1 Peter 3:9-4:6

### THE PATTERN OF CHRIST (3:9-12)

The previous passage (3:8) directed Christians how to relate to fellow-believers. Now (verse 9) Peter instructs them how to behave towards their persecutors. His words virtually repeat his instruction to the unjustly suffering slaves, 'Do not return evil for evil or reviling for reviling'. They are to take the unjustly suffering Christ as their example (see 2:21).

Peter is pointing his readers to Christ's example and teaching, though he does so in an indirect way. This he does (a) in verse 9 (where Christ's example is to be inferred), (b) in verses 10-12 in the citation from Psalm 34 (which is about Christ), and (c) in the next teaching, in verses 13-16 (where Christ's example and teaching is to be inferred).

3:9 *Do not return evil for evil*
*or reviling for reviling;*
*but on the contrary bless,*
*for to this you have been called,*
*that you may obtain a blessing.*
3:10 *For*
*'He that would love life and see good days,*
*let him keep his tongue from evil and*
*his lips from speaking guile;*
3:11 *let him turn away from evil and do right;*
*let him seek peace and pursue it.*
3:12 *For the eyes of the Lord are upon the righteous,*
*and his ears are open to their prayer.*
*But the face of the Lord is against those that do evil.'*

Peter's text falls into two natural divisions: (i) his appeal for non-vengeance towards persecutors (verse 9); (ii) his citation from Psalm 34 (verses 10-12).

(i) These unbelievers are directing 'malice' and 'reviling' (insults) towards believers. Their natural instinct would be to respond in kind, now or later.

Peter's response in verse 9 is particularly powerful. We note (a) his word 'for' means 'in place of', so that he is saying 'don't return evil *in place of* the evil you have received, insults *in place of* the insults you have received'; and (b) his '*but on the contrary*' expresses a direct reversal of returning evil for evil, the *blessing* of the persecutors.

Earlier Peter pointed unjustly suffering slaves to the 'example' of Christ, who:

> when he was reviled did not revile in return
> when he suffered did not threaten

Thus the unjustly persecuted believer (verse 9) like the unjustly suffering slave (2:23) is to think and behave in a non-vengeful way to those who act maliciously toward him.

Peter's words to slaves and persecuted citizens call to mind both the *actions* and the *words* of Jesus. At his crucifixion Jesus was reviled and insulted, but did not respond in kind, but prayed for those who were crucifying him (Luke 23:34-35).

This was entirely consistent with the Lord's earlier teaching:

> Love your enemies and pray for those who persecute you (Matthew 5:44).

Paul also knew this teaching of the Lord Jesus, which he gives in terms rather similar to those of Peter, 'Bless those who persecute you; bless and do not curse' (Romans 12:14). Paul writes something similar to the Thessalonians, 'See that none of you repays evil for evil, but always seek to do good to one another and to all' (1 Thessalonians 5:15).

Peter's encouragement to 'bless' the persecutor (verse 9b) prompts him to add, 'for to this you have been called, that you may obtain a blessing'. Here Peter goes back to the beginning of the letter and picks up the Father's 'call' (1:9) to them through the Gospel-word (1:25) to 'inherit' the blessing of an 'inheritance which is imperishable, undefiled and unfading' (1:4). Believers are able to bless those who persecute them because of the blessing they will inherit.

(ii) The writer's mention of 'obtaining a blessing' leads him to quote extensively from Psalm 34, which fulfils three purposes.

(a) Peter supports his appeal not to repay 'evil' by quoting Psalm 34.[24]

| Psalm 34 | 1 Peter 3 |
|---|---|
| v12 **For**, 'He that would love life and see good days, let him keep his tongue from **evil** | v9 do not return **evil** for **evil** |
| v14 let turn away from **evil** | |
| v16 the face of the Lord is against those who do **evil** | |

(b) The words from Psalm 34 can be seen as a prophetic anticipation of Christ. He inherited God's 'blessing' of 'life' and 'good days' (his resurrection) and the answer to his prayers because he kept 'his tongue from evil and his lips from speaking guile'. In short, God rewarded Christ with a 'long life' for his godly behaviour when unjustly treated. Believers suffering unjustly are to follow Christ's example.

(c) Peter picks up three words from Psalm 34 in the passage following, that is, 'evil' (in verses 13, 17), 'right' (and 'righteous' in verses 13, 14) and 'good' (verse 16).

---

24. Peter's words, 'you have tasted the kindness of the Lord' (2:3) are also derived from Psalm 34:8. The entire Psalm is about the goodness of God to his afflicted servants.

*Reflection on verses 9-12:* 'Payback' seems deep-rooted in human personality, whether of small children squabbling over a toy or local tribes fuming over some past insult. Nothing could be clearer, however, but that vengeance is not an option for believers in the face of evil done to them (verse 9). The only 'payback' (if we can use that word) is for believers to bless those who have done wrong to them.

That said, however, it does not necessarily rule out legal action where there is serious injustice. Legal action must be taken only for the sake of justice and not for the sake of revenge.

Non-revenge is a value in society that stems from apostolic teaching, which derives ultimately from the Lord Jesus Christ. This widely held value can break the cycle of 'payback', whether in families, between employees and employers, or between factions in society. Non-revenge provides the possibility of a civilized society and whether it knows it or not, this came from the teaching and example of Jesus.

## CHRISTIANS ON TRIAL (3:13-17)

This passage springs directly from its immediate predecessor where there are many references to 'evil' being done to believers (verses 9, 10, 11, 12). These are picked up in Peter's question in verse 13, 'who is there to *harm* ( = do evil to) you' which in turn grimly anticipates 'suffer' (verse 14a), 'fear' (verse 14b), be 'troubled' (verse 14c), 'abuse' (verse 16a), be 'reviled' (verse 16b) and 'suffer' (verse 17). The words reveal that Peter is writing to fearful and anxious people.

A keyword in verses 13-17 is 'good'—'zealots for good'[25] (verse 13), 'good behaviour' (verse 16) and 'doing good' (verse 17). 'Righteousness' (verse 14) appears to be a synonym for 'good'. What is the 'good' Peter speaks about? Is it 'goodness' as defined in the contemporary moralistic 'house-tables'? That seems unlikely in view of Peter's teaching in his 'house-table' (2:13-3:12). There he appealed

25. RSV has 'right' but it is the same word (Greek: agathos) that is translated 'good' in verses 16 and 17.

to various persons to 'be subject'—citizens to rulers, slaves to masters and wives to husbands, and to those who are unjustly treated not to seek revenge. Peter sums this up as 'your good behaviour in Christ' (verse 16) and it has an ultimate missionary intention.

But it is precisely these believers who are living in this 'good' way who are now so fearful and troubled. How will Peter address them?

3:13 *Now who is there to harm you if you are zealous for what is right?*
3:14 *But even if you do suffer for righteousness' sake, you will be blessed.*
*Have no fear of them, nor be troubled,*
3:15 *but in your hearts reverence Christ as Lord.*
*Always be prepared to make a defence*
*to any one who calls you to account for the hope that is in you,*
*yet do it with gentleness and reverence;*
3:16 *and keep your conscience clear,*
*so that, when you are abused,*
*those who revile your good behaviour in Christ*
*may be put to shame.*
3:17 *For it is better to suffer for doing right,*
*if that should be God's will,*
*than for doing wrong.*

In verses 13-17 we concentrate on Peter's three exhortations to his readers: (i) fear Christ, not the persecutor (verses 13-14); (ii) confess Christ even under interrogation (verse 15); (iii) ensure your behaviour is blameless (verses 16-17).

(i) While the possibility of 'harm' (better, 'evil') coming to these readers is real Peter assures them it is not absolute (verse 13). This is because the 'inheritance' promised them is secure, 'kept in heaven' for them (1:3-4; 3:9). As they face critics and enemies he urges them not to weaken in their 'zeal' for the 'good'. As Christ was subject to the authority of Pilate, so let them be subject to various authorities.

Indeed, the Christ whom they are now imitating pronounced his 'blessing' on and made his promise to those who 'suffer for righteousness sake' (verse 14a). Peter is adapting his Master's teaching for these persecuted disciples in northern Anatolia:

> Blessed are those who are persecuted for righteousness' sake, for theirs is the kingdom of heaven (Matthew 5:10).

So Peter comes to his strong appeal, 'have no fear of them[26], nor be troubled' (better, 'agitated'). These readers are deeply distressed; their fear is palpable. 'On the contrary', he says, 'in your hearts reverence Christ as Lord' (verse 15). He is saying just as your hope of heaven exceeds your apprehension of 'harm' (verses 13-14a), so also let your 'reverence for Christ' exceed your fearful distress (verses 14b-15a).

Peter's words, 'have no fear of them, nor be troubled but reverence Christ as Lord' are a direct adaptation of Isaiah's assurance to the people when Israel was facing invasion from the terrifying Assyrians:

> Fear not their *fear*, neither be troubled, but *reverence* Yahweh himself, and he shall be your *fear* (Isaiah 8:13).

Peter was a Jew and therefore a devout monotheist, committed to the thrice daily recitation of the *Shema* which declared, 'Hear O Israel, Yahweh our God is one...' (Deuteronomy 6:4). By speaking of Christ as 'Lord', whom they are to 'reverence', Peter is identifying Jesus Christ with Yahweh, the LORD of hosts, the creator of the world and the redeemer of his people. Peter's 'you have tasted that the Lord (Jesus) is kind' (2:3) similarly identifies Jesus with Yahweh since Psalm 34:8 says, 'Taste and see that *Yahweh* is good'.

Accordingly, let profound reverence for the majestic Lord Jesus Christ overshadow any fear inspired by man.

(ii) Since their hope of heaven exceeds their apprehension of 'harm' and their reverence for Christ exceeds their fear of the persecutor, let them be fearless in the face of interrogation.

---

26. Perhaps Peter is saying, 'Do not fear the fear that they inspire in you'. There is an echo in President Roosevelt's words spoken in World War II, 'we have nothing to fear but fear itself'.

Words from the legal arena like 'defence' and 'account' tell us that Peter has in mind a magistrate's trial. So we now see sinister developments in the regions this letter addresses. Initially former friends of these converts found it strange that they had discontinued their drinking binges and the accompanying sexual activities (see 4:3-4). Next these ex-friends have begun to spread evil rumours about them (2:12, 13) and to insult them in public (3:9, 16). Finally, it would appear, these enemies are bringing accusations against the believers in the courts.

For which crime are they accused? Most likely they were seen to be guilty of belonging to a sect that had a greater reverence for its founder Christ, than for the ruler of the world, the Roman Caesar ('Caesar' is a title of the Roman emperor; it does not refer to Julius Caesar). Peter's words reflect the situation of those times. Once the Gospel of Christ came out of Palestine westwards to the Graeco-Roman world, where Caesar reigned over all, the believers came under pressure to renounce Christ in favour of Caesar. 'These Christians are saying there is "another king", this person called Christ and they worship him and they will not worship Caesar' (see Acts 17:1-7).

Their accusers also believed they were guilty of awful vices which they committed behind closed doors. Tacitus, who was governor of Asia early in the next century, wrote that Christians were 'loathed for their vices' (*Annals* 15.44). This letter reflects current suspicion that believers were 'wrongdoers' (2:12, 14-15; 3:16-17; 4:15).

These matters would have weighed heavily on Peter who was writing from Rome (Babylon – 5:13), the seat of Caesar's power. He emphasises three connected points throughout this letter:

(a) Christians are to 'honour' the emperor; they are not to be seen to be disloyal – 2:17;

(b) Christians are to avoid any appearance of wrongdoing – 4:15;

(c) Christians must resolutely confess their allegiance to Christ – 3:15.

In regard to (c) let these believers prepare themselves for the likelihood of a trial and determine not to resile from their commitment to Christ. Confession of Christ is an absolute, a non-negotiable duty for the professed disciple.

Jesus said that the cross that the true disciple must bear is to publicly identify himself as a Christian, and that to be ashamed of him would warrant the reciprocal shame of God on the Last Day (Mark 8:34-38). Doubtless Peter remembered his own spectacular failure when he denied Christ in the High Priest's courtyard on the night his Master was arrested, and equally that Christ graciously reinstated him on the shores of Lake Galilee (John 18:15-27; 21:15-19). Peter's appeal, 'always be prepared to make a defence' has special poignancy in his own memory.

Significantly, the believers' defence is regarding the 'hope' they have. This is the 'living hope' of an imperishable inheritance, kept in heaven (1:3-4). Evidently, the believer's 'hope' made a great impression on unbelievers for which they demanded an 'account'.

Yet confession of Christ must be offered in ways that are consistent with Christ's known character, that is, 'with gentleness and reverence' (better, 'fear'). Christ declared himself to be 'gentle' (Matthew 11:29), and to 'fear' God, that is, he acted with profound awe of the Father. Accordingly, says Peter, we are to confess Christ gently and in the fear of God never proudly or arrogantly. Peter is calling for the confession of Christ in the manner of Christ.

(iii) Peter assumes that believers will be abused, based on misinformation (verses 16-17). He insists that Christians anticipate such insults and take precise care that they cannot be accused of any misbehaviour or crime.

Perhaps they will suffer for doing good deeds, if that is God's will. Painful though this will be, it is preferable by far to suffering as wrongdoers. On the day of judgment those who accuse them unjustly will be put to shame.

Once more we see in Peter's words the silhouette of Christ in his last hours. He did 'good' and did no wrong, yet he was reviled and suffered cruelly. Those who treated him unjustly will face the just judge and be ashamed of their actions. The same holds true for those who likewise unjustly and cruelly punish believers who are innocent of any wrongdoing.

*Reflection on verses 13-17:* Few Christians in the developed world are subject to persecution as Peter's readers were. Yet contemporary society criticises and rejects Christians for confessing Christ, whether in one's neighbourhood, school, university or workplace. We Christians feel pressure to water down our identity as believers and to remain silent when we should 'confess' that he is Lord and saviour.

Peter's words speak to us in our situation, even though it is different in many ways to Peter's readers. He calls on us not to be ashamed of Christ but to confess him. At the same time we are to do so humbly, as people who 'seek the welfare of the city'.

Are Peter's words 'always be prepared to make a defence' a call to engage in evangelism? The answer is, 'no, not directly'. Yet other parts of this letter do directly encourage believers to seek the salvation of unbelievers. The believers' 'good deeds' (of civic and social responsibility) are done with a view to 'winning' unbelievers to obedience to the word, something that will be apparent on the day of visitation (2:12). Here wives are the prime example of the expectation that believers will bend every effort to bring unbelievers to obedience to the Gospel-word (3:1-2). Accordingly, to resolutely confess Christ (3:15), though not in itself an act of evangelism, is inextricably connected with the sense of mission in the letter.

## CHRIST'S TRIUMPH OVER IMPRISONED SPIRITS (3:18-22)

The passage following is the most difficult in the letter.

Its core message is that Christ is now victorious over the forces of evil that might bring harm to the believers. The passage, then, makes best sense when seen in a context where Peter was assuring very frightened readers that their enemies can bring no evil against them (3:9, 13), that is, in the ultimate sense. Accordingly, let them give courageous witness to Christ, giving reverence to him alone (3:15), with no fear of their enemies.

We find the passage to be difficult for two reasons. First, Peter is using a form of exegesis that was then in vogue with Jewish Christians like him, but which is unusual to us today. They looked for events in the New Testament that corresponded with but superseded Old Testament precursors. They called the prefiguring events 'types' and the fulfilling events 'anti-types'. An anti-type 'fills the place of', or 'fulfils' a type. Thus in verse 21 we understand that the Genesis flood is the 'type' and 'baptism' is the 'anti-type', the fulfilment of the flood.

Secondly, it is not clear in verse 19 (a) who or what are 'the spirits in prison', and (b) what it means that the risen Christ 'went and preached' to them.

In regard to (a) Peter is alluding to the primeval events that preceded and necessitated the great flood (Genesis 6:1-8). A (forbidden?) sexual union had occurred between the sons of God (angelic beings) and the 'daughters of men' (ordinary women), whose offspring were called *Nephilim* (fallen ones). These *Nephilim* were the source of the appalling evil on the earth that prompted God to send the flood to wipe out all those infected with their evils. Only righteous Noah and his family were to be saved through the waters. According to popular belief God's watery judgment did not destroy the 'fallen ones', but imprisoned them for his ultimate judgment. These, most likely, are the 'spirits in prison'.

In regard to (b) the best sense (in our view) is that the slain but now risen and triumphant Christ 'went' to these evil beings and 'proclaimed' to them their imminent dethronement and condemnation.

The main alternatives to this theory are (i) Christ had preached through Noah back then, setting a courageous example for preachers now (for example, Augustine); (ii) Christ preached after his resurrection to people in hell offering a 'second chance', based on repentance (according to Goppelt). In our view neither of these explanations fits the context in which these words appear, that is to say, terrified believers facing hostile interrogation.

By so doing Christ has demonstrated his complete victory over evil beings, whether natural (like their present persecutors – see 4:4-6) or supernatural (like the imprisoned spirits). It is possible, but cannot be proved, that persecuted believers thought they had been oppressed by some alliance between their human enemies and these superhuman 'spirits in prison'.

3:18 *For Christ also died for sins once for all,*
*the righteous for the unrighteous,*
*that he might bring us to God,*
*being put to death in the flesh but made alive in the spirit;*
3:19 *in which he went and preached to the spirits in prison,*
3:20 *who formerly did not obey,*
*when God's patience waited in the days of Noah,*
*during the building of the ark,*
*in which a few, that is, eight persons,*
*were saved through water.*
3:21 *Baptism, which corresponds to this, now saves you,*
*not as a removal of dirt from the body*
*but as an appeal to God for a clear conscience,*
*through the resurrection of Jesus Christ,*
3:22 *who has gone into heaven and is at the right hand of God,*
*with angels, authorities, and powers subject to him.*

There are two main teachings in this complex passage: (i) Christ was effective in his atoning death and triumphant in his resurrection and ascension to announce his victory and the defeat of supernatural powers; (ii) therefore, let baptised believers be unafraid in the face of terrifying enemies.

(i) The Christ-story runs like a thread through this creed-like passage. Christ died; Christ was 'made alive in the spirit'; Christ 'has gone into heaven and is at the right hand of God''. Yet this is anything but a merely formal statement of belief. Christ is dynamic and effective in death, resurrection and ascension.

(a) Verse 18 is one of the most comprehensive statements about the meaning of the death of Christ to be found in the New Testament.

First, we note that it is preferable to translate verse 18a as 'Christ also *suffered* for sins' rather than 'Christ also died for sins'. The word 'also' picks up the previous verse where 'believers *suffer* for doing right' which in verse 18 Peter applies to Christ's sufferings. The theme of suffering is prominent throughout this letter (see 1:11; 3:17; 4:1, 12, 16, 19; 5:1, 10). Because Peter personally witnessed the 'sufferings of Christ' he can write that 'Christ...*suffered* for sins', a statement that is theologically *and* emotionally powerful (cf. 1:8).

Second, Christ's death in its effects was substitutionary and universal. It was *substitutionary* because he died 'in regard to sins', and 'in place of' others and it was *universal* because it was for the 'unrighteous', that is, all people. 'Righteous' Christ, the *unblemished* 'lamb' (1:19), 'stood in' for the 'unrighteous' in his sufferings at Golgotha.

Third, Christ's death was unique and final. The RSV translates a single Greek word as 'once for all', which points to the absolute and unrepeatable nature of Christ's death, as following texts illustrate:

> The death he died he died **once for all** (Romans 6:10)
> He appeared **once for all** at the end of the age (Hebrews 9:26)
> Contend for the faith...**once for all** delivered to the saints (Jude 3).

Fourth, God intended Christ's death to be the 'pathway' or 'means of access' to him. Peter employs a word that was used under the Old Testament dispensation for priests having access to the presence of God in the temple. Here, therefore, it points to God's people as a 'cleansed' priesthood coming directly into the presence of God (see also Romans 5:2; Ephesians 2:18; 3:12).

In short, therefore, while Christ's sufferings appear to be the ultimate, futile, humiliation and defeat, in reality through them the unrighteous of the world find acceptance and mercy in the presence of the holy God.

(b) In verse 19 Peter writes about the risen Christ and his journey to the 'spirits in prison'. This he states minimally, using contrasting words 'flesh' and 'spirit':

> Christ...being put to death in the *flesh*
> but made alive in the *spirit*
> ....he went and preached to the *spirits* in prison.

As noted above, the view taken here is that the risen Christ went to evil and imprisoned 'spirits' and proclaimed his saving death to them, not with a view to them being given a second chance, but to inform them of their imminent dethronement and final condemnation. Noah's preaching (compare 2 Peter 2:5) gave them opportunity to repent, but they declined to grasp that opportunity.

(c) In verse 22 Peter describes the final part of Christ's 'journey' following his death, in which 'he went into heaven'. There he is at 'the right hand of God', the place of absolute authority. From that time 'angels, authorities and powers', good and bad, are 'subject to him'.

Thus verses 18-22, which speak so powerfully of Christ's death, resurrection and ascension, give the reason believers are able to 'reverence Christ' in their 'hearts as the omnipotent Lord' (3:15), for that indeed is who he is. They have nothing to fear from supernatural powers since these are 'subject' to him. How much less is there to fear, therefore, from merely human persecutors?

(ii) The first teaching about Christ proclaiming doom to the imprisoned spirits (verse 19) is inseparable from the second, that is, baptised believers have been 'saved' (verses 20-21).

Peter is drawing on the Genesis account of the Flood story in which God saved 'righteous' Noah and his family. While in the Genesis story the water of the flood was the instrument of destruction of the wicked, in Peter's (typically Jewish) exegesis God saved those eight persons in the ark, 'through water'. Thus water is the 'type' that prefigures baptism, the anti-type that fulfils it. Accordingly Peter declares, 'baptism...now saves you' (verse 21a).

Peter, however, immediately clarifies a possible misunderstanding. It is not the water itself that saves, but that which accompanies and is signified by it, that is to say, 'the answer of a good conscience towards God, through the resurrection of Jesus Christ'. Peter is giving us a window into early Christian mission in which a person re-born through the Gospel-word would at his baptism speak of his now-forgiven conscience. That confidence of forgiveness only arose because of the death and resurrection of Christ.

Why does Peter tell this rather complex story of the flood? It must have been due to the pastoral reality in which many of these readers were frightened of the pain they were soon to face. Let them understand, however, that as genuine believers they were indeed 'saved', as his reminder of their baptisms told them. Furthermore, their majestic Lord is master of all the forces of life and death. They have nothing to fear, in the ultimate sense.

*Reflection on verses 18-22:* Despite its complexity this passage has a profound and important message to all believers in every situation. It is that the sufferings of our Lord in our place have saved us and brought us, forgiven into the presence of our holy God. Because Christ has risen and ascended in triumph it means that supernatural forces have no power in our lives, for they are subject to him. As well, we have nothing to fear from man so that we are free to make our good confession as disciples of Christ.

## PREPARE TO SUFFER (4:1-6)

This passage concludes the section that began with Peter's question, 'Who is there to do evil[27] to you?' (3:13) and directs our attention (a) to those who do the evil (verses 3-6), and (b) believers who suffer under the evil (verses 1-3).

27. RSV translates 3:13 as 'Now who is there to *harm* you...?' which doesn't quite capture the force of the original Greek kakoo, 'do evil'.

Peter has just declared that the crucified, risen and ascended Christ has gone victoriously to the right hand of God with 'angels, authorities and powers subject to him'. This triumphant Christ is now 'ready to judge the living and the dead', including those who 'do evil' to believers.

Peter makes two contrasts: (a) between *flesh* and *spirit,* and (b) between the *past* and the *present.*

The first (a) is *spatial* contrasting human existence *down here* (flesh) with God's world *up there* (spirit).

| | |
|---|---|
| spirit | God's world |
| \| | |
| flesh | Humanity's world |

The opposites 'flesh' and 'spirit' pick up the earlier reference to Christ who was 'put to death in the *flesh*' but who was 'made alive in the *spirit*' (3:18) where he paraded his dominance over '*spirits* in prison' (3:19).

Peter continues this 'flesh versus spirit' contrast in verses 1-6, but now as it applies to humanity. God's purpose in sending the Gospel to men 'in the flesh' (including the wicked who persecute) is positive, that is, that they will 'live in the spirit' according to the will of God (verse 6). In short, Peter looks for them to be re-born and live ethically.

The second contrast (b) is *temporal* contrasting former wicked lives of the readers before re-birth through the Gospel-word with their present lives that are under persecution.

**Past | Present**

'the time that is past' | 'the rest of the time'

Peter repeatedly contrasts their re-born present with their wicked past (for example, 1:14, 18; 2:9).

We note that the spatial and the temporal contrasts are connected, and the connector is the Gospel. The Gospel separates the wicked past from the godly and penitent present; the Gospel is the 'high speed lift' out of 'the flesh' (the sinful world) up to (the world of) the Spirit (God's holy presence).

'Spirit'

g
o
'the time that is past' s 'the rest of time'
p
e
l

'flesh'

While Peter uses the word 'spirit' initially for the realm of God in contrast to the realm of sinful 'flesh', it is evident that we are also meant to think of the 'spirit' as the 'Holy Spirit'. This means that those re-born by the Gospel, who now live 'in the Spirit', according to the will of God must not live 'in the rest of time' as they used to live 'in the time that is past'.

4:1 *Since therefore Christ suffered in the flesh,*
*arm yourselves with the same thought,*
*for whoever has suffered in the flesh has ceased from sin,*
4:2 *so as to live for the rest of the time in the flesh*
*no longer by human passions but by the will of God.*
4:3 *Let the time that is past suffice for doing what the Gentiles like to do,*
*living in licentiousness,*
*passions,*
*drunkenness,*
*revels,*
*carousing,*
*and lawless idolatry.*
4:4 *They are surprised that you do not now join them in the same wild profligacy, and they abuse you;*
4:5 *but they will give account to him who is ready to judge the living and the dead.*
4:6 *For this is why the gospel was preached even to the dead,*
*that though judged in the flesh like men, they might live in the spirit like God.*

This passage falls into three sections: (i) how the re-born are now to live (verses 1-2); (ii) how the 'Gentiles' continue to live wickedly and as persecutors and what will happen to them (verses 3-5); and (iii) God's positive purpose in sending the Gospel (verse 6).

(i) Peter often refers to Christ's 'sufferings' (1:11; 2:21, 23; 3:18; 4:13), which he personally witnessed (5:1). Because these believers belong to him and bear witness to him they 'share in the sufferings of Christ' (4:13). Thus Peter speaks many times of the 'sufferings' of believers (1:6; 2:19, 20; 3:14, 17; 4:15, 19; 5:9, 10). Such sufferings range from verbal abuse and public insult (2:12; 3:16) to likely death (4:15-16). In these circumstances believers may be tempted to hide their identity as believers, something they must not do (see 3:15). Accordingly (verse 1a), Peter tells them to 'arm' themselves with the 'same mind' as Christ who did, indeed, suffer.

Peter's use of military language, 'arm yourselves' (verse 1b) is an indication of the enmity they experienced.[28] Peter used similar imagery earlier when he wrote that 'passions of the flesh *war* against the soul' (2:11). Clearly, to live as a believer in that culture was a severe struggle.

The basis for readiness to suffer is that 'whoever has suffered in the flesh has ceased from sin' (verse 1c), a statement that is not easy to understand. The following sentences (verses 2-3) that call for the re-born life to be radically unlike the wickedness of the former life assist us to grasp Peter's meaning. Becoming a believer means becoming a confessor (3:15) and becoming a confessor means becoming a persecuted sufferer (3:17; cf. v4 'they blaspheme you'). In turn, becoming a sufferer means truly becoming a penitent. Peter is saying that Gospel re-birth and persecution went together. Who would go back to the bad old ways of the 'time that is past' when one had suffered as a confessor of Christ? Suffering as a confessor focuses the mind for repentance.

This verse has been misunderstood to encourage asceticism as means of deliverance from sinful practices.

28. Peter's verb hoplizÿ is related to 'hoplite', a heavily armed Greek soldier.

Throughout history men and women plagued with guilt about sexual passion and other 'cravings' of the 'flesh' have sought escape through various means of self-inflicted suffering. Some have gone to extremes, living as hermits or wearing clothing that pierced the skin in their efforts to rise above their sexual appetites. Peter is not writing to encourage such practices, but to point out that suffering arising from persecution means that Gospel re-birth in practice means leaving wickedness behind.

In verse 2 Peter states the purpose of those sufferings (in v1), which amplifies what it means to 'cease from sin'. That purpose is:

| | | | |
|---|---|---|---|
| *that* | you | | |
| | no longer | live | by the passions of men |
| but | | | |
| | in the time that is left in the flesh | | |
| | | [live] | by the will of God |

Peter's time notes 'the time that is left' and 'no longer' will soon stand in contrast with 'the time that is past' (verse 3). In that earlier 'time' they lived by the promptings of 'the passions (cravings) of men', when they were 'ignorant' of God (see on 1:14; 2:11).

(ii) The believers are God's 're-born Israel' (1:3, 23) living among the 'Gentiles' (cf. 2:11). As 're-born' they must 'no longer' live as these 'Gentiles' do, and as they used to live before the Gospel-word brought them new life. Peter's sketch of that behaviour is similar to Paul's descriptions of Gentile vices (see for example, Romans 1:18-32; 13:13; Galatians 5:19-2; Ephesians 5:3-5) and could easily be corroborated even in non-Christian writers of that era.

These vices fall into three categories: sexual practices (licentiousness, passions, revels), indulgence in alcohol (drunkenness, carousing) and the worship of the gods (lawless idolatry). These are overlapping vices. In modern secular societies sexual licence and abuse of alcohol (and drugs) are frequently connected. In Peter's day pagan worship in temples (including at festal occasions), sexual licence and binge drinking were frequently connected. Earlier Peter referred to 'futile ways inherited from your fathers' (1:18). Graeco-Roman culture, for all its high achievement, was a culture of futility, morally speaking.

These patterns of behaviour identify the original readers as predominantly Gentiles. The people of the Old Testament had frequently fallen into idolatry, but this had long since been left behind. By New Testament times Jews, including those who lived in the Diaspora, scrupulously avoided idolatry and the sexual practices of the Gentiles among whom they lived. They would not eat food sacrificed in the temples nor even enter the house of a Gentile.

True, those who brought the Gospel-word to northern Anatolia were Jews, whether returning pilgrims baptised by Peter at Pentecost in Jerusalem, or Peter himself, or his 'son' Mark. Doubtless many of the early believers there were likewise Jews. By the time Peter wrote the letter, however, a majority of the readers appear to have been Gentiles.

It is clear from verse 4 that these godless 'Gentiles' are a source of persecution. The 're-born' ones previously engaged in the same drinking bouts, sexual licence and futile idol-worship. Former companions in these activities are now 'surprised' (better, shocked or startled) that believers do not 'join in' with them in the 'same flood[29] of dissipation'. In reaction to the spiritual and moral re-birth of previous friends, these 'Gentiles' abuse (better, blaspheme) them (cf. 2:11; 3:16; 4:14). It is likely that this social rejection was the precursor of the more official persecution (3:15).

But let there be no misunderstanding. These wicked ones who are also persecutors will not avoid the displeasure of Christ, their judge. True, at this present time believers are compelled to give an 'account' for their 'hope' to a human judge (3:15). But the time is coming when the situation will

---

29. Greek anachusis can mean 'outpouring' perhaps recalling the flood that God sent to a godless world that anticipated the present wickedness (Gen 6:5-7). RSV has 'profligacy'.

be reversed and they, the accusers, will have to give their 'account' to the risen and ascended Christ, who is 'ready' to judge the living and the dead.

(iii) Peter concludes this passage (verse 6) with a weighty observation:

| | | | | |
|---|---|---|---|---|
| a. | For this is why the gospel was preached to the dead | | | |
| b. | that they may | be judged | in the flesh | according to man |
| c. | but | live | in the Spirit | according to God. |

We need to understand two things about this difficult verse. First the 'dead' are most likely Peter's metaphor for those wicked ones portrayed so graphically in the previous verses.

Second, we note that verse 6b and 6c are 'legs' that are set in parallel, but as opposites (technically called 'antithetic parallelism'). Thus in the following 'pairs' we observe items that correspond but as opposites:

| | | |
|---|---|---|
| 'judged' | corresponds with but is opposite to | 'live' |
| 'flesh' | corresponds with but is opposite to | 'Spirit' |
| 'man' | corresponds with but is opposite to | 'God' |

Verse 6b 'that [the dead] may be judged in the flesh according to man' is quite difficult to understand. Perhaps the key to understanding it is to understand the leg verse 6c, which is saying that when the Gospel is preached to the 'dead' (the wicked) they begin to 'live' by the power of 'the Spirit' in a new relationship with 'God'. In other words, they are 're-born'. Accordingly, the problematic leg 6b is saying the opposite, that is, when the 'dead' (the wicked) reject the Gospel they are 'judged' (by God) 'in the flesh' and confined to the realm of wicked 'man' excluded from a relationship with God. In other words, they are lost.

God's desire, however, is the redemption of the wicked.[30] It was for that purpose the Gospel-word was preached in

30. Peter is not advocating the view that God gives a 'second chance' to the deceased.

those five Roman provinces, which has led to the re-birth of those previously morally 'dead' Anatolians who are now believers (1:3, 12, 25; 2:1).

The present unrepentant 'dead' (the wicked) in Peter's generation correspond with the unrepentant wicked in Noah's generation, who are the 'spirits in prison' awaiting their doom (3:19). This means that the fate of the unrepentant 'dead' (the wicked) in the New Testament era is as dreadful in prospect as the fate of the 'spirits in prison' from the era of the flood. Yet while there is life there is hope. The present unbelievers (the 'dead') may still be 'saved' and 're-born' (unlike their counterparts, the 'spirits in prison', who have no hope).

Peter may be implying a contrast with the great flood that swept away the wicked of that era, with the exception of Noah and his family. Under the Gospel dispensation, however, God seeks the salvation of all, not just a few, and he seeks their redemption through the good news of Jesus Christ.

*Reflection on 3:13-4:6:* Peter wrote these words under the inspiration of the Holy Spirit to comfort his readers in a time of suffering arising from persecution. He assured them that Christ was stronger than any human enemy and that they were safe in his strong hands, that is, in the ultimate sense. Therefore, let them not be silenced by the enemies around them. Since Christ has now dominated and dethroned supernatural forces how much less do they have to fear from merely human persecutors? Peter would agree with his fellow-apostle Paul that the struggle is not ultimately against 'flesh and blood' (mere humans) but against 'spiritual hosts of wickedness in the heavenly places' (Ephesians 6:12).

Nothing has changed fundamentally since Peter's day. The forces of spiritual evil continue to use human agencies to silence the witness of Christians and to discredit them. There is a threefold challenge here that is as relevant today as it was when Peter was writing: (i) be unashamed and unafraid to confess Christ and to declare yourself to be a disciple; (ii) be prepared to leave behind the sins of the former manner of life; and (iii) be committed to living a 'good manner of life' in Christ, being subject to the authorities ordained by God.

## CONCLUSION

The entire passage 3:9-4:6 is really Peter's portrayal of Christ, his behaviour and his words. He suffered for the truth of God, though without having committed any crime. He did not threaten or abuse his persecutors, but retained a dignified silence as he handed over his life to God for his justice on the last day. In all of this Christ is the perfect template for believers to copy as they face injustice. Their Christ-like behaviour will provide them with opportunity to 'give a reason for the hope' they have. Thus we see once more the connection between replicating Christ and proclaiming Christ. The imitation of Christ has a missionary intent, that is, for believers to speak about the Lord whose behaviour is being imitated.

At the same time, the triumphant victory of the risen and ascended one means that the believer is able to face evil with the confidence that Christ has conquered evil. There is nothing to fear except fear itself. The greater 'fear' of Christ brings liberty and joy in the face of human evil.

# 4

# Stand Firm: The end is near

## 1 Peter 4:7-5:11

'The end of all things is near' (4:7) signals the beginning of the final part of the letter. Peter had referred to end-time matters earlier ('salvation ready to be revealed in the last time...at the revelation of Jesus Christ' 1:5, 7; 'set your hope fully on the grace that is coming to you at the revelation of Jesus Christ' 1:13). Indeed, immediately before this passage Peter spoke of the readiness of Christ to judge the living and the dead (4:5).

Yet from this point onward there is a continuing emphasis on the end ('the time has come for judgment to begin' 4:17; 'the glory that is to be revealed' 5:1; 'the unfading crown of glory' 5:4; 'in due time he may exalt you' 5:6).

Consistent with these 'end-time' references Peter makes many 'appeals' to his readers. This is to be expected since the approach of the 'end' calls for their perseverance and an ever-greater concentration on their relationship with God and with one another.

Accordingly, Peter appeals to them in regards their relationships—with one another (4:7-11), with outsiders (4:12-19), with their leaders (5:1-5), and with their persecutors (5:6-11).

This section, therefore, is a fitting end to the letter. We recall that it began with their beginnings, that is, with their 're-birth'. So now, appropriately, it concludes with their 'end'. Between their re-birth and their end believers are to be witnesses to God's grace to them, and they are to do so in the face of ferocious opposition.

In quite brilliant ways, therefore, Peter has narrated the

believers' 'story' as it has unfolded from start to finish, while at the same time 'appealing' to them as to how that 'story' *must* unfold from start to finish. This is why so much of the letter is devoted to Peter's 'appeals' to his readers.

## LOVING RELATIONSHIPS IN THE CHURCHES (4:7-11)

In this passage there are many points that correspond with Romans 12-13.

| | 1 Peter 4 | | Romans 12-13 |
|---|---|---|---|
| v7 | the end...is **at hand** | 13:12 | the day is **at hand** |
| | keep...**sober** for your prayers | 12:3 | think with **sober** judgment |
| v8 | hold unfailing your **love** | 12:9 | let **love** be genuine |
| v9 | practice **hospitality** | 12:13 | practice **hospitality** |
| v10 | as each has received a **gift** | 12:6 | having **gifts** that differ |
| | **serving**[31] one another | 12:7 | if service, in our **serving** |
| v11 | whoever **speaks** | | he who **teaches**, in his teaching |

The repeating words in the two passages cannot be coincidental. What is the explanation? Perhaps Peter is depending on Paul's text, or vice versa? Yet in other respects the texts are quite dissimilar. Therefore the most likely reason for the repetitions is that Paul and Peter are each depending on an independent and earlier written tradition directing congregational life in the early churches. On this account, each writer has adapted the tradition for the needs of their respective readers.

Peter leaves his readers in no doubt as to the importance of the 'last things' (technically called eschatology). He begins by referring to the 'end of all things' and concludes with the 'glory' of God. His fourfold 'appeal' regarding behaviour in the churches sits between these powerful references to the end.

*4:7 The end of all things is at hand;*
*therefore keep sane and sober for your prayers.*

---

31. Greek, diakoneo, 'serve', contra RSV 'employ.'

4:8 *Above all hold unfailing your love for one another,*
*since love covers a multitude of sins.*
4:9 *Practice hospitality ungrudgingly to one another.*
4:10 *As each has received a gift, employ it for one another,*
*as good stewards of God's varied grace:*
4:11 *whoever speaks, as one who utters oracles of God;*
*whoever renders service, as one who renders it*
*by the strength which God supplies;*
*in order that in everything God may be glorified through Jesus Christ.*
*To him belong glory and dominion for ever and ever. Amen.*

Everything in the passage flows out of (i) Peter's bold assertion that 'the end of all things is at hand' (verse 7a), after which (ii) he 'appeals' to them to pray sanely (verse 7b), to love one another (verse 8), to practise hospitality (verse 9), and to exercise the gifts of speaking and serving (verses 10-11a). The fulfilment of these appeals is (iii) for the glory of God (verse 11b).

(i) The words 'the end of all things is at hand' evoke images of wild-eyed, bearded men holding doomsday placards announcing 'the end is nigh'. Is this Peter's message here?

For a start, we must note that 'all things' refers to the present broken and dysfunctional state of the world where life is typically futile and people are imprisoned by their 'passions' (1:14, 18; 4:3-4), where human glory is as transient as withering grass (1:24), where masters are cruel to slaves (2:18), husbands overbearing to wives (3:6), and unbelievers remorseless in hounding believers (2:15).

Next, in that regard Peter's word 'end' means 'goal' (not doom) and that goal is the 'perfection' or 'completion' of all that is disjointed and fractured in this present dispensation.

Finally, we observe that 'at hand' does not mean that the end is 'at the door' so much as 'now in sight' or 'coming into a state of nearness'. This is the same word Jesus used in declaring, 'The kingdom of God is *at hand*' (Mark 1:15). The ship is coming because we can see the smoke from the funnels and make out its shape in the distance as it approaches. The burden of Peter's words is that the 'end' is definitely drawing near, but is not so imminent that we can predict the precise time of its arrival. Nonetheless, that does not diminish the importance of his appeals.

(ii) Since the 'end' will mean 'perfection' or 'restoration' it follows logically that believers should conduct themselves with one another appropriately in the meantime. In short, Peter is saying that church life is to be a preview of the 'end' when God will make all things 'perfect'.

(a) Sharpened expectation of the end has from time to time inspired apocalyptic fanatics to advocate extreme behaviour. For example, in 1993 David Koresh and eighty Branch Davidian followers suffered a fiery end in Waco, Texas.

By contrast, Peter urges his readers (verse 7b) to be 'sane' (better, self-controlled) and 'sober for their prayers' (cf. 1:13). Believers, both individually and together, will draw near to God soberly, in adoration, intercession and thanksgiving. In answer to their prayers God will strengthen them to fulfil his good purposes set out in the following appeals Peter will make.

(b) His pre-eminent appeal comes in verse 8, '*Before all things* love one another strenuously' (cf 'love one another earnestly' 1:22). In their struggle to stand firm in their sufferings for the truth (5:9), 'before anything else', they must 'love one another'. Doubtless Peter recalled Jesus' teaching on their last night together that the mark of their genuineness as his disciples was to love one another as he loved them, especially in a situation of persecution (John 13:34; 15:19).

That love will be expressed primarily in forgiving others in the community of faith, which Peter states figuratively as 'love covers a multitude of sins'. There will always be a need for forgiveness, given and received, due to the persistence of sin in the human heart. This is especially true in married and family life but also in congregational life.

Perhaps, though, Peter is conscious that times of stress (including persecution) often bring out the worst in people so that they say and do things they do not typically do or say. Hanging in together under persecution will depend on mutual understanding and love, expressed as forgiveness. Perhaps this will also be directed to those who have failed to confess Christ (cf. 3:15). Peter may be reflecting on his own failure and Christ's merciful love shown to him on the beach of Lake Galilee (John 21:15-19).

(c) Various New Testament writings call for the practice of hospitality (see Romans 12:13; Titus 1:8; Hebrews 13:2). Local congregations met in private homes; hospitality was needed to provide a place for believers to meet. Travelling missionaries were accommodated in private homes; hospitality was needed to look after penniless visiting preachers and prophets. There were no hostels for orphans, widows, the elderly or the unwell, and hospitality was needed for these folk.

Significantly, giving hospitality is one of the qualifications needed in a church elder (1 Timothy 3:2) and for a woman to be enrolled for the church to care for her on becoming a widow (1 Timothy 5:10).

Hospitality could be expensive and inconvenient. It was also susceptible to abuse and exploitation. The *Didache*, which was likely written several decades after First Peter, warns of visiting prophets who exploited the hospitality provided (*Didache* 11-13). In the mid-second century the pagan writer Lucian writes humorously about a charlatan named Peregrinus who made himself wealthy by exploiting Christian hospitality (Lucian, *On the Death of Peregrinus*, 11-16). Accordingly, Peter urges that hospitality be offered 'ungrudgingly' (better, without murmuring).

(d) Peter's three previous appeals were implicitly directed to individual hearers of the letter. He directs his fourth appeal (verse 10) explicitly to 'each' of them.

Peter calls them 'stewards', 'each' of whom has 'received

a gift' (from God). In that culture a wealthy householder entrusted a 'steward' with money to distribute for provisions and wages, and so on, for the administration of the household. Here, Peter is calling ordinary members 'stewards' who are to dispense God's gifts to others in the congregation.

The close verbal connection here between 'grace' *(charis)* and 'gift' *(charisma)* matches their close theological connection. God reveals his 'varied grace' to people, which in turn becomes 'concrete' in them as a heaven-sent gift, to be used for the benefit of others. Peter's grace/gifts language here bears close similarity with Paul's teaching about ministry in the body (see 1 Corinthians 12:4-11; Romans 12:3-8).

Like Paul, this writer insists that God gives his gifts to his people for them to use in 'serving' (Greek: *diakoneō*) one another in the community of faith. In that sense all members are 'deacons' serving one another. God does not give the 'gifts' in order that the person so 'gifted' will draw attention to himself. These activities and ministries are just that, 'gifts'. Humility about oneself and deep love for others are the only bases for the exercise of gifts (as Paul also taught in 1 Corinthians 13:1-3).

Paul went into a lot of detail describing the gifts. In Romans 12:3-8 he mentions seven activities and in 1 Corinthians 12:27-30 he lists eight activities. In verse 11a, however, Peter mentions only 'speaking' and 'serving'. Most likely, 'speaking' includes teaching the tradition (written and oral) and prophesying and encouraging inspirationally from that tradition. 'Serving' included almsgiving and the care of widows and orphans and other needy people (in that pre-welfare society).

This practical help became a feature of early Christianity. Less than a century following this letter Justin Martyr wrote about Christian charity:

> This collection was for the succour of the orphans and widows, and those who through sickness or any other cause, are in want, and those who are in prison, and the strangers sojourning among us, and in a word takes care of all who are in need (*Apology* 1.66).

The same development is on view half a century later in Tertullian's comment.

> Even if there is a chest of a sort, it is not made up of money paid in entrance fees, as if religion were a matter of contract. Every man once a month brings some modest coin—or whenever he wishes, and only if he does wish, and if he can; for nobody is compelled; it is a voluntary offering. You might call them the trust funds of piety. For they are not spent upon banquets or drinking parties; but to feed the poor and to bury them, for boys and girls who lack property and parents, and then for slaves grown old and ship-wrecked mariners; and any who may be in mines, islands or prisons, provided it is for the sake of God's school, become the pensioners of their confession (*Apology* 39:1-6).

This practical care of one another spilled out to the needy in the wider community and mightily impressed the watching world at that time. Indeed, a Pagan emperor like Julian (fourth century) attempted unsuccessfully to get the Roman state to replicate Christian 'good works'. The modern 'welfare society' has evolved from the Christian beginnings reflected in this passage.

(iii) As the passage began with the 'end', so it will conclude (verse 11b). There, though Peter's reference is to the 'glory' of God. When the 'end' finally arrives all people will be dazzled by the glory of God. Gone will be the wickedness and the sadness of the world; all that will be visible will be the moral brightness of God.

In the meantime, however, believers have the privilege and the opportunity to 'illuminate' the invisible God by their prayerful dependence on him and the 'strenuous' love expressed in forgiveness and in serving one another by word and deed.

Peter concludes with a powerful ascription of praise to Jesus Christ. Earlier Peter declared that God had 'raised him from the dead and gave him glory' (1:21) and that he had 'gone into heaven to God's right hand, with angels, authorities and powers subject to him' (3:22). Now Peter states that 'glory and dominion belong to him forever' (verse 11b). This Christ who has suffered for sins, as an example of godly patience in the face of terrible injustice, is now vindicated in the place of supreme honour and authority.

The modern reader senses that in hearing these words of devotion, love and praise we are hearing these churches worshipping their heavenly Lord and Saviour.

*Reflection on 4:7-11:* When this intense statement about life together within the fellowship of the church is added to the earlier passage (1:22-2:10) it becomes clear that Peter cared deeply about these churches. This is not surprising in light of Peter and the other disciples' experience with Jesus, who taught them and showed them how to love one another. After the resurrection Peter helped shape the church in Jerusalem as a genuine loving and caring community. This letter indicates that Peter upheld the same high ideals for the community life of the churches in Anatolia. We know from Paul's letters that he was utterly committed to similar ideals.

It is clear from the New Testament letters that many churches fell far short of these ideals, as they do now. It would be a mistake to be overly romantic about the churches of that era. The fact that the New Testament letters need to say so much about church life is commentary enough.

Nonetheless, it is worth noticing the stark contrast between the wickedness in Anatolia (and Rome) as sketched by Peter (4:2-4) and the behaviour Peter calls for in the church (4:7-11). Much of wider Graeco-Roman society was characterised by 'passions' (cravings) and freewheeling, self-centred behaviour involving drunkenness and sexual promiscuity. Even if the reports of the behaviour of the highest echelons of society are exaggerated, it appears that Graeco-Roman world was quite debauched. (It would be incorrect, however, to characterise it as universally debased since there were likely many people who lived temperately). Those who followed the teachings of the moralists did not give themselves in loving service of others, regardless of their rank or status. Life in the church, however, was to be others-centred and love-directed in the spirit of a servant.

Few things are more important to God than the welfare and character of his churches. God's will is that they are shaped by Peter's words in this letter. Because when that happens, even if imperfectly, God himself is authentically portrayed. Accordingly, pastors and people must work at shaping our churches in the ways Peter has outlined.

One final reflection relates to Peter's promise of the 'end', which many today now doubt. Indeed, Peter's second letter addressed those self-same doubts about the promise of his coming ('Where is the promise of his coming?' 2 Peter 3:4). Peter was a witness to the bodily resurrection of Jesus from the dead. He was in no doubt that as Jesus had departed into heaven so, one day, he would return. Meanwhile, said Peter, you must see that his delay is motivated by divine mercy, to provide greater opportunity for repentance for all people (2 Peter 3:9).

## JUDGMENT: NOW AND LATER (4:12-19)

Peter sets before the readers the example of Christ (2:21), but also on several occasions his teachings. In the following passage he quotes from the Sermon on the Mount:

| 1 Peter 4:14 | Matthew 5:11 |
| --- | --- |
| If you are **reproached** | **Blessed** are you |
| **for the name of Christ**, | when men **revile** you |
| you are **blessed** | and persecute you |
| | and utter all kinds of evil |
| | against you falsely, **on** |
| | **my account** |

Peter does not attribute this teaching to the Lord, nor is it an exact quotation but rather an adapted and shortened version. But there can be no doubt that Peter is appealing to a 'word' of the Lord.

There are references to persecution and suffering earlier in the letter (see 1:6-7; 2:12, 15; 3:13-17; 4:4). Yet Peter heightens and intensifies the theme of suffering and its challenge to the commitment of believers:

12 *Beloved, do not be surprised at the fiery ordeal which comes upon you*
*to prove you, as though something strange were happening to you.*
13 *But rejoice in so far as you share Christ's sufferings,*
*that you may also rejoice and be glad when his glory is revealed.*
14 *If you are reproached for the name of Christ,*
*you are blessed, because the spirit of glory and of God rests upon you.*
15 *But let none of you suffer as a murderer,*
*or a thief,*
*or a wrongdoer,*
*or a mischief-maker;*
16 *yet if one suffers as a Christian, let him not be ashamed,*
*but under that name let him glorify God.*
17 *For the time has come for judgment to begin with the household of God;*
*and if it begins with us,*
*what will be the end of those who do not obey the gospel of God?*
18 *And 'If the righteous man is scarcely saved,*
*where will the impious and sinner appear?'*
19 *Therefore let those who suffer according to God's will*
*do right and entrust their souls to a faithful Creator.*

The passage is warmly encouraging, while addressing the readers facing a difficult future. Peter addresses his 'beloved' readers in respect of two imminent and daunting realities—the coming fiery ordeal (verse 12) and the beginnings of the judgment of God (verse 17). Various challenging scenarios are introduced by 'if', followed by a contrastive 'appeal' (introduced by 'but') as to how they should respond.

(i) Peter addresses his readers warmly as 'Beloved' (for the second and last time in the letter—see 2:11). God called his Son 'beloved' (Mark 1:11) and this is likely the reason believers are also said to be 'beloved by God' (Romans 1:7). God's approach to lost humanity is love-based and those who have been drawn to God by that love are to love one another.

Peter now warns them of the 'fiery ordeal' that is 'coming' to them (and to 'the brotherhood throughout the world' 5:9).

It is likely that Peter is referring to the great fire that destroyed three quarters of Rome in AD 64 for which Nero 'scapegoated' the Christians, many of whom he crucified and set alight (Tacitus, *Annals of Imperial Rome* 15.44).

Peter would have assumed that this 'fiery ordeal' would spread to the provinces, including in northern Anatolia. This explains why he warns them, 'do not be surprised...as though something strange were happening to you' (verse 12).

He observes that God's purpose for the 'fiery ordeal' was to 'prove' believers, that is, to 'strengthen' them further so as to confirm their genuineness (see 1:6-7). Earlier Peter had observed that one who has suffered persecution for the faith has 'ceased from sin' (4:1).

Based on this frightening reality Peter appeals to them to 'rejoice', not because they will suffer *per se*, but that because they will 'share in Christ's sufferings' (verse 13). Peter is speaking about only one kind of suffering, suffering flowing from persecution because of the believers' confession of Christ. Peter is saying that the believer will rejoice because he is recognised as a true disciple of the Lord. The sufferings of Jesus at Golgotha have overflowed from him and reached his faithful, confessing people throughout the world. This being so, how glad will they be when his glory is revealed. Peter often connects suffering with glory in regard to Christ (1:11; 1:18, 21; 5:1), and Christians (1:6-7; 5:10).

(a) Peter now introduces the first of his three 'if' scenarios, that is: '*if* you are reproached[32] for the name of Christ' (verse 14a). Peter declares that person 'blessed' because he is sharing in the overflowing sufferings of Christ

32. Note the various terms Peter uses for abusive language against Christ and Christians:

| | | Christ | Christians |
|---|---|---|---|
| 'speak against' | (katalaleō) | | 2:12; 3:16 |
| 'revile' | (loidoreō) | 2:23 | [3:9] |
| 'abuse' | (epēreakō) | | 3:16 |
| 'blaspheme' | (blasphēmeō) | | 4:4 |
| 'reproach' | (oneidizō) | | 4:14 |

and therefore 'the Spirit of glory and of God is resting upon him' (verse 14b).

This first 'if' scenario is followed by his contrastive appeal, '*but* let none of you suffer as a murderer, thief, wrongdoer or mischief-maker'. The first three are crimes in any culture and bring legally based punishment. 'Mischief-maker' refers to someone who meddles in a person's private concerns, earning that person a bad reputation.

These negative commands are closely connected with Peter's earlier emphasis on being 'subject to every human institution' (2:13-14). To 'be subject' to those who hold public office also demands respect for morally based laws. Any breach of such laws must mean that commitment to society's leadership is hollow, if not hypocritical.

Unbelievers will be quick to criticise and make fun of Christians for any inconsistency, great or small. Believers must ensure that there is only one 'crime' of which they are guilty, that is, they follow Christ and are publicly identified as his disciples.

(b) Peter's second 'if' scenario relates precisely to suffering 'as a Christian'. The way Peter writes suggests that such suffering is actual not hypothetical. Let that person not be 'ashamed' but, as Peter said earlier, 'rejoice' (verse 13a).

This second 'if' scenario, like the first, is followed by a contrastive appeal, '*but* under that name [Christian] let him glorify God' (verse 16b). God is glorified by the way a man or woman lives. In the kingdom of God 'glory' will be visible brightness. Now, however, 'glory' is a metaphor for 'bring credit or praise to someone'. Children 'glorify' parents by behaving in ways that bring praise for their effective parenting. By analogy God is 'glorified' when those who are known as 'Christians' behave like Christ, that is, morally, humbly, patiently, truthfully and compassionately.

Were Christians, however, to be guilty of murder, theft, wrongdoing, mischief-making or similar blatant actions then God would not be glorified. There are numbers of prominent sportsmen and sportswomen who are known to be

Christians. If such people break the rules of the game or deliberately injure other players, the general reaction would be, 'I don't think much of your God if that is the way one of of his children behaves.'

(ii) The second reality is that 'the time has come for judgment to begin with the household of God' (verse 17). Peter's word 'time' (Greek: *kairos*) does not mean 'time' in general but a 'special time' in the unfolding purposes of God. Peter sees that 'time for judgment to begin' as having come in the 'fiery ordeal' already mentioned (verse 12).

What, then, is this judgment? It is not the day of final judgment since this will occur at the 'revelation of Jesus Christ' (1:13).

Nonetheless, that 'last judgment' begins within history whenever the Gospel-word is welcomed or rejected. The issues of eternal salvation are settled in the here and now as the word of God is heard and received or heard and rejected. 'Judgment' begins at times of persecution because believers are driven to decide whether to continue as believers or to turn their backs on Christ. Likewise, that 'judgment' begins when the persecuted begin to engage in revenge, following the ways of the world and not the example of Christ (see 2:21; 3:9). Persecution brings pressure to de-convert—it is a 'special moment' that corresponds in an opposite way to 're-birth' through the word. The judgment of God will be revealed later but it actually occurs right now, at the 'time' when the decision to continue as a believer or to commit apostasy is made.

Because of this Peter reflects momentarily on the plight of those 'who do not obey the gospel of God' (verse 17b). He is thinking of those many in Anatolia who have, indeed, heard that Gospel but who have not obeyed it (see 2:8; 3:1). Obedience to the Gospel is the mark of the believer and the means of his re-birth (cf. 1:14, 22). Those who have heard and disobeyed, however, have already sealed their own fate.

(c) Peter's third 'if' scenario ('If the righteous man is scarcely saved, where will the impious and sinner appear?')

is stated as an adapted quotation from Proverbs 11:31. New Testament writers often cite Old Testament texts to illustrate what they are saying. However, this does not mean that every last word in the quotation is to be pressed. Peter is quoting the Proverb to emphasise the danger faced by the unbeliever. He is not saying that the 'righteous' are 'scarcely saved', as if believers' salvation hung in the balance.

Peter again makes a contrastive appeal:

> Therefore let those who suffer according to God's will
> do right and
> entrust their souls to a faithful creator.

Note that the suffering here is due to persecution. Peter is saying that God is sovereign in the world and in history and that persecutions are within and part of that 'will'. God is not the source of evil and suffering, but he permits it to happen, within his larger purposes.

Times of persecution may inspire erratic behaviour among believers. Earlier Peter had insisted on self-control and sobriety for prayerfulness in such difficult times (see 4:7b). Now he calls for them to 'do right', that is, to continue to live morally by the precepts and example of Christ and continue to 'be subject' to 'every human institution' (2:13). Further, he encourages them to 'entrust' (better, hand over) their souls to the Creator who is faithful.

Peter is pointing us to the example of Christ (see 2:24). When Christ was arrested, put on trial and crucified he did 'right and entrusted his soul to his faithful creator'. The persecuted believer is to do the same, knowing that God's final judgment will be just and that in the meantime God is faithful. Soon Peter will put that another way, encouraging them to 'humble themselves under the mighty hand of God' (5:6).

*Reflection 4:12-19:* This passage calls for sober reflection, in particular because God's judgment begins *now* and depends on how we hear and obey the Gospel. Persecution is like evangelism in reverse because it presses on us to de-convert, to commit apostasy. In that moment God's judgment, indeed, has been made, and it has been made negatively. This is the plight of those who have heard and disobeyed the Gospel.

Peter, however, writes with positive intent. He is appealing to us to be 'approved' through the testing fires of persecution, in which the Spirit God will rest upon us. 'Continue to do what is right and to trust the faithful creator', he is saying. He calls on us not to shrink from confessing Christ, but to ensure that we cannot be accused of any crime.

Few Christians pass through life without trials, even if they are not the extreme kind that faced Peter and his readers. Trials associated with accidents, health, relationships (especially within families) and money force us to reflect on whether or not we truly believe in God and his fatherly love of us. These are times when, though we may be 'tested' hard, God himself draws near to us. Often that 'drawing near' will come through the loving support of others. Seeing another person in difficulty challenges us to be good friends to them in their times of need. Elders in the local church have a special responsibility in providing care and support for members who face times of trial.

## PETER'S APPEAL TO PRESBYTERS (5:1-4)

Despite Jesus' explicit commission, 'As the father has sent me, even so I send you' (John 20:21), Peter and six other disciples had returned to their previous occupation as fishermen. Peter had publicly disowned Christ (John 18:15-18, 25-27) and he compounded that sin by disobediently returning to his old job. Jesus pointedly addressed Peter by his pre-disciple name, 'Simon son of John', asking whether Peter loved Jesus 'more than these [fishermen, boats, nets, etc]'. Being reassured by Peter, Jesus said 'shepherd my sheep' (John 21:16)—the Greek literally means 'tend as a shepherd' and the noun 'shepherd' has been translated below in a verbal sense to bring out the meaning. Jesus' command, 'shepherd my sheep' became deeply imprinted in Peter's memory and evidently also became a fundamental instruction among the apostles. This is clear from Peter's words in 5:2, and also in Paul's direction to the presbyters (elders) of Ephesus in Acts 20:28.

| 1 Peter 5:2 | Acts 20:28 |
| --- | --- |
| **Presbyters**.... | [**Presbyters**] |
| **over-see** the **flock of God,** | ...take heed...to all the **flock** |
| **shepherding** [them] | in which the Holy Spirit |
| | has made you **over-seers,** |
| | **shepherd** the church **of God,** |

The common elements (presbyters, over-see[r], shepherd, flock of God/church of God) are striking. Did Peter copy these words from Acts, or vice versa? It is more likely that Peter and Paul were drawing from an early common tradition that had been formulated for guidance to local church leaders.

Peter (with John) was the leader of the earliest Christian mission, which was directed to the land of Israel, centred on Jerusalem. As Peter established congregations in those earliest times it was obvious that these churches needed local leaders. These were called 'elders' or 'presbyters' (Greek: *presbuteroi*), a term most likely copied from elders in the synagogues (cf. Acts 11:30; 15:2). When Paul began his missions among the Gentiles in southern Anatolia and Greece he, too, appointed local leaders and called them 'presbyters' ('they appointed elders for them in every church' Acts 14:23).

We conclude that the 'office' of presbyter became universal within early Christianity. Since Peter addresses 'presbyters' in the churches of northern Anatolia it follows the leaders in the churches in Rome were also known by that name.

The two passages above (1 Peter 5:2 and Acts 20:28) teach a triangular relationship between 'presbyter', 'shepherd' (or pastor from Latin: *pastor* –shepherd) and 'over-seer' (Greek *episkopos* evolved through Latin and Old English to 'bishop' and literally means 'seeing over' or 'seeing from above'). These three words from 1 Peter 5:2 and Acts 20:28 appear often within the New Testament.

*Presbyter* denotes a position of leadership within a congregation; *shepherd* points to the caring nature of that leadership; *over-seer* implies seeing the people 'from above'. (Perhaps we can imagine a shepherd watching over the whole flock and looking out for those who are tending to wander away from the flock.)

5:1 *So I exhort the elders among you,*
*as a fellow elder and a witness of the sufferings of Christ*
*as well as a partaker in the glory that is to be revealed.*
5:2 *Tend the flock of God that is your charge,*
*not by constraint but willingly, as God would have you do*
*not for shameful gain but eagerly,*
5:3 *not as domineering over those in your charge*
*but being examples to the flock.*
5:4 *And when the chief Shepherd is manifested*
*you will obtain the unfading crown of glory.*

This passage is one of a number in which an apostle sets out the responsibilities of leaders of local churches, for example Paul's charge to the presbyters of Ephesus, noted above (see Acts 20:17-35). Paul also directed his junior colleagues Timothy and Titus about the qualities they should look for in 'bishops' in local congregations (1 Timothy 3:1-7; cf. 5:17-22 and Titus 1:5-9).

There are three natural parts to this short passage: (i) Peter's appeal to presbyters (verse 1), (ii) how they should and should not 'shepherd the flock' (verses 2-3), (iii) promising them 'an unfading crown of glory' for doing so (verse 4).

(i) This is the second time that Peter 'appeals' to (or exhorts) his readers (2:11; cf. 5:12). The earlier 'appeal' was directed to all his readers whereas here it is addressed to the 'elders' (while the Greek literally means an older man, 'presbyter' is a better translation because it captures the idea of a man who held a responsible position in the church).

Peter is an *apostle* (1:1) who had *seen* the Lord (cf. 1:8), who was a *witness* to the *sufferings of Christ.* He is writing to provide for the ongoing care of the churches beyond the life span of apostles like him (Paul did the same in his letters to Timothy and Titus). The apostles were the critical bridge between Jesus and the post-apostolic era. By the time Peter wrote (in the mid-60s) the apostolic age was rapidly passing.

It appears that Peter was killed soon after writing this letter. The apostles' choice of and directions to these presbyters would be critical to the future of post-apostolic Christianity. Every generation of believers needs faithful and capable presbyters, but no generation was as needy as in those years following the apostles.

Peter was a presbyter as well as an apostle. He calls himself 'fellow-presbyter' for several reasons. First, Peter had been the leading presbyter in the Jerusalem church, combining that role with his travelling ministry in the land of Israel (see for example, Acts 9:31-32). Perhaps, at the time of writing he held a similar position among the church (or churches) in Rome.

Secondly, Peter wants to identify with these Anatolian presbyters. Peter was a historical 'witness to the sufferings of Christ'; they are reliving those 'sufferings' in the persecutions that have fallen on them locally. He will be a 'partaker in the glory to be revealed' (Peter often refers to the 'revelation' of the future glory of God (1:5, 7, 12, 13, 4:13); they will likewise 'share' in that glory, receiving its 'unfading crown' (see v4). Implicit in Peter's words is his warm encouragement for the presbyters to imitate him in faithfulness and perseverance. What has been true of him is also to be true of them.

(ii) Peter's exhortation to presbyters to 'shepherd the flock' has a rich background in Old Testament thought and in the teaching of Jesus.

God was the Shepherd of his people (Psalm 80:1), who led and cared for them by means of 'shepherds' like Abraham, Moses and Joshua (Numbers 27:15-19), but in particular the shepherd-king, David (2 Samuel 5:1-4). David and other 'shepherds' failed in their vocation so God promised to send a 'new David', a true shepherd who would save and provide for the people (Jeremiah 23:5-6; Ezekiel 34:23-24). Aware of this Jesus declared himself to be the 'good shepherd' (John 10:11; Luke 15:1-7). His instruction to Peter, 'Feed my sheep' (John 21:15-17) shows that he foresaw a great future 'flock' that would need shepherds. Peter's words are the outworking of Jesus' redemptive mission for the world. God's people need pastors!

Peter explains that these presbyters 'shepherd the flock' by 'over-seeing them'. This implies that the presbyter will be aware of the circumstances of individual members, not least in times of persecution when believers may feel pressure to abandon the faith. The shepherd imagery suggests that the presbyter should be aware that some sheep tend to stray, while others are stragglers, and some struggle to keep up with the flock.

The moral character of the presbyter is critical to the welfare of the flock, as Peter now establishes by three powerful statements. In each statement there are matching opposite keywords, namely: constraint/willingly, shameful/eagerly, domineering/as examples.

(a) Shepherd the flock...

| | |
|---|---|
| not by constraint | but willingly, as God would have you do[33] |

Peter's words imply that presbyters were chosen and appointed by the apostle (initially) and then by the congregation. Presbyters were not volunteers. Reference to 'not by constraint' suggests that many found this 'calling' to be onerous. It is likely that offering 'hospitality' was a task that typically fell to presbyters ('practise hospitality ungrudgingly' 4:9). As well, the presbyter would be a prime target in times of persecution.

God, however, seeks *willing* servants, not passive and grudging ones. God is active (not passive) and has a servant's mind. Accordingly his people, presbyters in particular, are to be active and willing to serve one another. We may reasonably extrapolate from Peter's appeal that presbyters were to be active, energetic, cheerful and generous. Field

33. Some ancient authorities omit, 'as God would have you do'.

Marshall Eisenhower once commented that 'long faces don't win hard battles!'

(b) Shepherd the flock...

| | |
|---|---|
| not for shameful gain | but eagerly |

Peter is not saying that presbyters should not be paid. Certainly the local leaders in the Pauline mission were to be paid (see Galatians 6:6; 1 Timothy 5:17-18) and Paul expected that visiting apostles, likewise, were to be paid for their ministry (1 Corinthians 9:3-12). What Peter is saying is that a lack of eagerness and an absence of willingness means that the motive for being a shepherd is really financial, a matter for 'shameful gain' (cf. Titus 1:7). Motive is everything!

(c) Shepherd the flock...

| | |
|---|---|
| not domineering over those in your charge | but being examples to the flock. |

The words 'those in your charge' mean the people allocated to the care of the presbyter, that is, 'the flock'. This prompts the question, 'who allocated the congregation to the presbyter?' Most likely it was the apostle or evangelist who originally gathered the congregation. Beyond that time, however, Peter gives no clue as to who was responsible for appointing local presbyters. In an ultimate sense Peter may be remembering the Lord's words to him, 'Shepherd *my* sheep' (John 21:16). In that sense it is the chief shepherd (Christ) who assigns an under shepherd to care for a 'flock' of *his* people.

The presbyter, who is Christ's under-shepherd, must not 'domineer' the flock. 'Domineer' is literally 'lord it over', a word Jesus used to describe ruthless and oppressive Roman governors ('those who...rule over the Gentiles *lord* it over them...' Mark 10:42). Jesus, however, declared that he 'came to serve, and to give his life a ransom' (Mark 10:45). Though he was 'Lord' he lived and died as a 'servant' of his people. Jesus the 'good shepherd' was radically different from the false shepherds of Israel—corrupt kings, priests and prophets—who ruled the people 'with force and harshness' (Ezekiel 34:4).

Accordingly, presbyters are to be 'examples to the flock' not as 'lords' but as 'servants'. Paul also said, 'What we preach is not ourselves but Jesus as Lord, with ourselves as your *servants* for Jesus' sake' (2 Corinthians 4:5). The presbyters' example in serving the members will mean that member serves member, recalling Peter's words that 'each' is to 'serve one another' (4:10).

Christ set the ultimate example of 'serving', an example to be followed by presbyters, who in turn set that example to members, making a congregation a serving community. Clearly, though, presbyters are the 'bridge' between Christ and the church. Above all they need to be shaped and formed by Christ's example as the great servant.

(iii) Peter concludes by assuring the presbyters that when 'the chief shepherd is manifested' they will receive 'an unfading crown of glory' (verse 4).

The pre-resurrection Jesus described himself as the 'good shepherd' (John 10:11) who had 'come to seek and to save the lost' (Luke 19:10). New Testament writers continue to apply shepherd language to the risen and glorified Jesus. The writer to the Hebrews calls him 'the great shepherd of the sheep', that is, in relation to all people everywhere (Hebrews 13:20). Peter, however, speaks of Christ in relation to other shepherd-presbyters, as 'the chief (or first) shepherd'. Christ is the Shepherd above the shepherds, the shepherd and over-seer of souls (2:25).

This 'chief shepherd' will be 'manifested' or made visible (this is another way of referring to '*revelation* of Jesus Christ', 1:13) at the end to gather his flock from all nations. Jesus said, 'I have other sheep, that are not of this fold; I must bring them also, and they will heed my voice. So there shall be one flock, one shepherd' (John 10:16). Twice Peter uses the word 'make manifest': (a) Christ *was* 'made manifest at the end of times' (1:20), and (b) he *will be* made manifest at 'the end of all things' (verse 4). Between those twin peaks (incarnation and revelation) Christ suffered for sins but was raised alive and glorified at God's right hand so that at his second manifestation he will be, indeed, glorious.

At his glorious 'manifestation' his faithful presbyter-shepherds will receive a 'garland' or 'wreath'. In Peter's day this was a reward honouring an athletic champion or military hero. Yet most likely Peter's allusion is biblical rather than cultural (cf. Isaiah 28:5 'The Lord of hosts will be a crown of glory and a diadem of beauty'). In early Christianity the 'wreath' was an established metaphor for God's special recognition of faithfulness.

All believers share the same salvation (cf. 1:3-4), yet there is special recognition for faithful service. The returning, glorious Christ will 'crown' those presbyters who have been 'willing', 'eager' and 'examples' of service to others.

*Reflection on verses 1-4:* Sadly, two millennia of Christian history have revealed many church leaders who have not served the people but lorded it over them. This has been as true in the Protestant tradition as it has been in the Roman Catholic and Orthodox tradition. Like those false shepherds in Israel they 'ruled' their people 'with force and harshness'.

Those who belong to the reformed and evangelical tradition (as I do) will see the 'ministry of the word' as central. Yet a servant mind expressed in love for the members of the 'flock' must undergird that expository approach to ministry. Negative motives like those mentioned by Peter (a sense of begrudged 'constraint', 'desire for shameful gain', a 'domineering' spirit) and others like them rob the presbyterate of Christ-like qualities. A biblical ministry that is expressed with passion and skill, yet which lacks warmth of heart and a generous and willing spirit betrays the God whom it seeks to commend. The people to whom the word comes inevitably hear that word from a human mouth. Those who hear that word cannot help reflecting whether that mouth speaks credibly, like Christ himself, with genuine loving concern for the salvation of the hearers.

## HUMILITY (5:5)

Next Peter addresses the 'younger' and 'all' within the congregation. This follows logically from his exhortation to the presbyters (5:1-4).

*5:5* *Likewise you that are younger be subject to the elders.*
*Clothe yourselves, all of you, with humility toward one another,*
*for 'God opposes the proud, but gives grace to the humble'.*

(i) In verse 5a Peter instructs the younger members of the congregation to 'be subject' to the presbyters.

As noted earlier to 'be subject' does not mean 'be obedient' in a servile sense but implies a willing acceptance of God-given authority. The principle of personal discretion still applies for those 'subject to' others. That might imply total compliance, unless there were an issue of morality or conscience.

Peter is saying that just as presbyters are 'subject' to God-given principles of 'shepherding' (5:2-3), so too members of the flock are to respect their leaders, in particular the younger members.

Peter is expressing a broad based teaching. As an apostle Paul expects church members to accept and follow his teachings ('If anyone refuses to obey what we say in this letter, note that man and have nothing to do with him, that he may be ashamed. Do not look on him as an enemy, but warn him as a brother' 2 Thessalonians 3:14-15). Paul also called on congregations to accept the authority of their leaders ('[R]espect those who labour among you and who are over you in the Lord and admonish you, and esteem them very highly in love because of their work' 1 Thessalonians 5:12). Likewise the Letter to the Hebrews teaches, 'Obey your leaders and submit to them...' (Hebrews 13:17). Members of the early churches were to respect their leaders and be subject to their godly discipline, a principle that still applies.

(ii) In writing 'But all of you' Peter qualifies his injunction 'be subject' to the 'younger'. Otherwise the readers may have been left with a rather bleak patriarchal vision of church life where the young inevitably bend to the will of their presbyters. Peter's direction to 'all' members, presbyters included, to 'clothe' themselves with 'humility toward one another' shifts the emphasis away from the 'top down' imagery connected with the injunction, 'be subject'. In short, the congregation needs to be characterised by a member-to-member respect, based on humility.

In appealing to readers (metaphorically) to 'clothe' themselves with humility Peter is articulating a common apostolic tradition (Romans 13:12; Ephesians 6:11, 14; 1 Thessalonians 5:8). Peter echoes almost exactly Paul's words to the Colossians (Colossians 3:12). Paul lists humility among four other moral qualities whereas Peter singles out humility. The 'humility' tradition pre-dated Paul arising originally from Jesus, who declared himself to be 'meek and *humble* in heart' (Matthew 11:29).

Peter buttresses his appeal for humility by citing Proverbs 3:34. That proverb contrasts the 'humble' with the 'proud'. Whereas the 'humble' have a sober and realistic view of themselves, the 'proud' are arrogant and self-important, viewing themselves above others. Pride opposes God but once the Gospel is welcomed it gives way to humility towards God and other people. The unrepentant 'proud', however, are in a grim situation. God the Almighty One is 'ranged against' them at this time, as he will also be at the end.

*Reflection on verse 5*: Humility is fundamental to the life of the believer. Humility before God in regards human mortality and wickedness is a necessary precursor to welcoming the good news of God's mercy shown in the sufferings of Christ for our sins. The 'proud' will never be able to hear that message since they are blinded by their own self-importance. That, however, is not the end of humility. As we progress in the Christian life we become aware of the depths of our self-centredness and our capacity to injure even those who are closest to us. As the prophet declared, we are to 'walk humbly with our God' (Micah 6:8).

Equally there is the challenge to be humble in relation to one another. Once again, any innate sense of superiority will be a barrier to relationship with others in the congregation.

Among the sources of pride are wealth, academic attainment, official position, physical prowess and attractiveness. A reality check is needed for those endowed with such things. After all, no human achievement is possible apart from the strength, the gifts and the opportunities that God provides.

John Calvin's words are worth hearing. In his *Institutes of the Christian Religion* he wrote '[I]f you ask me concerning the precepts of the Christian religion, first, second, third...always I would answer "humility".'

## TRUST GOD, RESIST THE DEVIL (5:6-11)

This powerful passage has many links with other parts of the New Testament.

(a) Even the casual reader will notice the similarities of the text with James 4:6-10.

| James 4:6-10 | 1 Peter 5:5-9 |
|---|---|
| | 5 for **'God opposes the proud, but gives grace to the humble'.** |
| 6 But he gives more grace; therefore it says, **'God opposes the proud, but gives grace to the humble'.** | 6 **Humble yourselves**...under...**God** that in due time he may **exalt you**. |
| | 9 **Resist** [**the devil**], firm in your faith, |
| 7 Submit yourselves...to God. **Resist the devil** and he will flee from you. | |
| 10 **Humble yourselves** before **the Lord** and he will **exalt you** | |

The similarities (quotation from Proverbs 3:34 'humble yourselves' before/to the Lord/God; 'resist the devil') are such that we must conclude that Peter and James are drawing upon the same early tradition. At the same time, however, these writers apply the tradition to their own individual situation.

(b) Peter is echoing traditions found in Paul's First Letter to the Thessalonians.

| 1 Thessalonians 5 | 1 Peter 5 |
|---|---|
| 6 ...let us keep awake and **sober**[34] | 8 Be **sober** , be **watchful** |
| 23 May the **God** of peace<br>sanctify you wholly;<br>and may your spirit and<br>soul and body be kept sound<br>and blameless at the coming<br>of our Lord Jesus Christ. | 10 The **God** of all grace<br>who has **called** you<br>to his eternal glory in Christ<br>will himself restore<br>establish, and strengthen<br>you. |
| He who **calls** you is faithful<br>And he will do it. | |

Both passages come near the end of their respective letters. The injunctions to watchfulness and sobriety are identical (in reverse word order) and the final prayers to God are quite similar in intent if not in precise wording.

(c) Peter's exhortation about 'anxiety' echoes Paul's encouragement to the Philippians. Behind Paul's and Peter's appeal is (Greek/LXX) Psalm 54:23 'Cast thy worry upon the LORD' and Jesus' words, 'do not be anxious...' (Matthew 6:25-34).

| Philippians 4:6 | 1 Peter 5:7 |
|---|---|
| Have no anxiety about anything | Cast all your anxiety on [God] |

It is clear that in verses 6-11 Peter is echoing traditions found also in James' letter and Paul's First Letter to the Thessalonians and his Letter to the Philippians.

Yet Peter's application of the tradition to his readers' situation, unlike James' and Paul's applications, is painful in the extreme. His references to suffering his readers face are more direct than any to date in his letter. If God will exalt them ultimately it is because he has 'abased' them beforehand, that is, through the hostile acts against them in Anatolia.

---

34. The apostolic encouragement 'to watch' comes from Jesus' words (for example, Mark 13:32-37).

Put another way, they have an inveterate adversary, the devil whom Peter portrays as a ferocious predator on the prowl seeking someone to kill and eat. This is very grim indeed for the original readers. They will survive (in the ultimate sense) only as they willingly submit to God, on one hand, while immovably resisting their supra-human adversary, on the other.

6 *Humble yourselves therefore under the mighty hand of God,*
*that in due time he may exalt you.*
7 *Cast all your anxieties on him, for he cares about you.*
8 *Be sober, be watchful.*
*Your adversary the devil prowls around like a roaring lion,*
*seeking some one to devour.*
*Resist him, firm in your faith, knowing that the same experience of suffering*
*is required of your brotherhood throughout the world.*
10 *And after you have suffered a little while,*
*the God of all grace, who has called you to his eternal glory in Christ, will himself restore, establish, and strengthen you.*
11 *To him be the dominion for ever and ever. Amen.*

The prospect of the readers' impending sufferings dominates this passage. Note that Peter begins (verse 6) and ends (verse 11) with reference to God's 'might' (the connection is clear in the Greek, but is lost in translation). The reminder of God's power and his reliability is a major encouragement to the readers, vulnerable as they were to the devil's attacks.

The passage falls into four parts: (i) Peter's appeal to them to rely on God (verses 6-7), (ii) his appeal to them to resist the devil (verses 8-9); (iii) his promise that God will restore, establish and strengthen them (verse 10); (iv) his ascription of praise to God for his eternal 'dominion' (verse 11).

(i) Peter makes his 'appeal' to rely on God in two parts.
(a) 'Humble yourselves *therefore*...' (verse 6) picks up the appeal for humility toward one another in the previous verse. Here, however, he appeals, 'Humble yourselves...under the

mighty hand *of God*'. 'The hand of God' is God's powerful involvement in the world, to deliver his people. It was a term used for God's 'mighty' deliverance of his enslaved people from Egypt. See for example, Exodus 3:19-20 [God said to Moses] 'I know that the king of Egypt will not let you go unless compelled by a mighty hand. So I will stretch out my hand and smite Egypt...' (cf. Exodus 6:1; 13:3, 9, 14, 16; Deuteronomy 9:26, 29; 26:8).

This was (and is) a comforting reminder of God's invincible sovereignty over events and circumstances to people under the threat of dire trouble, as Peter's original readers were.

Behind Peter's words we see the silhouette of Christ, wrongfully accused and (apparently) at the mercy of evil persecutors Caiaphas and Pontius Pilate. Though mocked and tortured, he remained in dignified silence, putting his trust in God the just judge for vindication on the Last Day. Christ is the model *par excellence* of the believer who is being persecuted, one who 'humbled' himself 'under the mighty hand of God' and who looked for the 'due time' that God would 'exalt him'.

(b) Peter's encouragement to submit humbly under God's 'mighty hand' is closely connected with his further exhortation to 'cast all worry' (fear) 'on God'. In fact, the two are inseparable. One cannot truly humble oneself under God's protection while racked with fear. Handing over fear to God and humbling oneself under his mighty hand happen together.

Earlier Peter encouraged these sufferers to 'do right and entrust' their 'souls to a faithful creator' (4:19). In verse 7 Peter is even more direct. To those who are being reviled, abused, insulted and dragged before magistrates Peter says 'cast' (as a burden) 'all worry' on God. This is because God 'cares for you', as Jesus so clearly taught (Matthew 6:25-34). Our God, whose 'hand' is 'mighty' is at the same time our 'dear Father' (cf. 1:17). Jesus trusted his Father in adversity, showing us how to live when we are burdened with worry.

(ii) Familiarity with these words may blunt the sense of terror that believers would have been felt, both in 'Babylon' (Rome) and in the Anatolian provinces. The world wide 'brotherhood' (cf. 2:17) must have felt on the edge of a global assault against them.

The hostility of the masses and of Roman officials toward believers was likened to a roaring lion, a savage predator. If you have heard lions roar you will know how frighteningly loud the noise is!

It is unlikely that Peter is referring to Christians being sacrificed to lions in gladiatorial arenas since that practice seems not to have begun until the next century. It is more likely he is echoing Psalm 22 in which the godly sufferer cried, 'They open their mouths wide at me, like a ravening and *roaring lion*' (verse 3). Jesus quoted the first sentence of Psalm 22 when he was crucified ('My God, my God why have you forsaken me?' Matthew 27:46). Peter seems to be connecting the suffering Christ with the suffering Christian.

Peter is attributing the persecution to supra-human forces, as does Paul (Ephesians 6:12 'We wrestle not against flesh and blood...'). In the shadows is the sinister figure of the devil, inspiring the anger of former drinking and womanising friends and the subsequent magistrates' trials. Here we must note that Peter's word 'adversary' means 'legal prosecutor', recalling the 'law court' situation earlier (3:15 'be prepared to make a *defence*').

These persecuted ones have done no evil, only good. They are loyal and responsible citizens. Their only crime was to bear the name 'Christ'. The assault on such people, therefore, could only be attributed to supernatural evil.

There is an end-time sense to Peter's words. The 'fiery ordeal' that is coming (4:12) signals that 'judgment' is about to begin with the household of God (4:17). As noted earlier, persecution is like evangelism in reverse since it applies pressure on believers to de-convert, that is, to commit apostasy (see 4:17). Persecution, therefore, is a 'special time'.

For this reason Peter uses eschatological terms like 'be sober...watchful'. These were the terms Jesus used when awaiting the return of the Son of Man (see Mark 13:35-37).

What does Peter mean by 'Resist [the devil], firm in your faith' (verse 9)? In the setting of this letter it means the same as, 'Always be prepared to make a defence to anyone who calls you to account for the hope that is in you' (3:15). To resist the devil, therefore, means stand firm as a Christian confessor, whatever the cost.

Peter was calling on believers in Anatolia, and no doubt in Rome, to lock arms and face the supra-natural foe. He exhorted the international brotherhood of disciples to stand firm in their loyalty to the Lord Jesus Christ.

(iii) In verse 11 Peter contrasts the brevity of their suffering (a little while) with the endless eternity of heaven (his eternal glory). Human life is transient and brief like 'the grass that withers' and 'the flower of the field that falls' (1:24). By contrast their inheritance is 'imperishable' and it is secure, 'kept in heaven for them' (1:3-4). In contrast with this 'eternal glory', their sufferings for Christ will only be 'for a little while'.

Meanwhile, they have 'humbled' themselves under the 'mighty hand' of God, having 'cast' their 'worry on him' knowing that 'he cares for' them (verse 6-7). Let them be comforted in their understanding that from first to last he is 'the God of all grace' (Cf. 2 Corinthians 1:3 'the God of all comfort'), 'who gives his grace to the humble' verse 5. By his 'great mercy' they have been re-born to 'a living hope' (1:3), their 'salvation' (1:5, 9). This was the 'grace' that *was* to come (1:10), the grace that *does* come (5:5), and the grace of God that *will* come (1:13; 3:7; 5:12). In the midst of life, including its pain, God surrounds them before and after with his grace.

This mighty God, who is the God of all grace, will himself draw near to them, both in Rome and the Anatolian provinces. They are but 'aliens and exiles', ordinary people who are frightened about what will happen to them. But God will 'restore' those who have failed, 'support' those who are weak, give 'strength' to those who are faint hearted and 'establish' a firm foundation under those who are wavering.

(iv) Peter rounds off this passage with his reassuring ascription to God: 'to him be dominion (better, 'might') for ever and ever' (verse 11). They are fragile and vulnerable but God is mighty. They are 'flesh that perishes', but God is eternal (for ever and ever).

*Reflection on verses 5-11:* Peter is writing about the severe difficulties facing his readers in the northern Anatolian provinces. At the same time, his words likely reflect the situation in Rome itself (Babylon) from which he is writing.

Peter emerges from this text as a true leader and 'shepherd' of God's scattered and suffering people. Having failed dramatically, Peter was now the 'rock' Jesus said he would become. In the intervening decades he proved God to be trustworthy and had, as a result been strengthened within himself to lead and care for Christ's sheep.

Peter writes out of his experience rather than from a tenured academic position in a university or a secure ecclesiastic cloister. He was a humble fisherman who was spurned as uneducated by the religious establishment of his day. Yet he had listened to and observed his Master, seen him arrested and killed and had been the first (male) witness to his resurrected life. Peter had experienced the life-changing power of the Spirit and seen the power of the Gospel to 're-birth' and redeem the lost. We the readers do well to heed his appeals.

# 5

# Final Greetings

## 1 Peter 5:12-14

In closing Peter mentions someone who has assisted him in writing the letter, sends greetings from colleagues and pronounces a final benediction upon his readers.

### PETER AND SILVANUS (5:12)

*5:12 By Silvanus, a faithful brother as I regard him,*
*I have written briefly to you,*
*exhorting and declaring that this is the true grace of God;*
*stand fast in it.*

(i) Peter states that he wrote to these Anatolian believers 'through Silvanus'. This prompts two questions: (a) Who was Silvanus, and (b) what does 'through Silvanus' mean?

(a) Silvanus (as Paul also calls him in 2 Corinthians 1:19) is the same person whom the book of Acts calls Silas. Silvanus was a prophet from Jerusalem who became a prominent figure in early Christianity. In *ca. AD* 49, James the president at the Jerusalem Council, instructed Silvanus (with Judas Barsabbas) to write the Council's decisions (likely from Aramaic into Greek), in an encyclical letter for the Greek-speaking congregations in Syria and Cilicia (Acts 15:19-30).

A measure of Silvanus' competence in Greek was Paul's choice of him as companion on the next missionary tour. It appears that, like Paul, Silvanus was a Roman citizen (Acts 16:37). Silvanus accompanied Paul through Syria and Cilicia, Asia, Macedonia and Achaia, regions that were linguistically Greek but politically Roman (Acts 15:40-18:5).

Silvanus, with Paul and Timothy, was co-founder of the church in Corinth and a co-author with them of Letters to the Thessalonians that were written from Corinth in *ca.* AD 50 (2 Corinthians 1:19; 1 Thessalonians 1:1; 2). After this we lose sight of Silvanus until the 60s when he appears alongside Peter in Rome. Where had he been in the meantime—perhaps in Northern Asia Minor, ministering to some of the churches whose members are addressed in First Peter?

The evidence from the New Testament provides a 'window' through which we catch glimpses of Silvanus from the later AD 40s until the mid-60s. Silvanus was a Jew, likely from Jerusalem, Aramaic and Greek-speaking, a Roman citizen and an experienced and trusted colleague of both Paul and Peter.

Peter states that he regarded Silvanus 'as a faithful brother', which probably means that while many of the readers knew him, he was not universally known. By these words Peter is commending Silvanus, in particular to those who do not yet know him.

(b) What, then does Peter mean, 'I have written to you *through* (Greek: *dia*) him'?

Peter's reference to writing 'through' another person has a parallel in the book of Acts, in that situation coincidentally where we first meet Silvanus.

The Jerusalem council entrusted Silvanus with the task of translating (and most likely interpreting) their decisions in a letter written in Greek for the churches in Syria and Cilicia. The book of Acts describes this in terms similar to Peter's in his circular letter written 'through' Silvanus to the Anatolians. The similarity only emerges from the Greek text:

> They sent Judas called Barsabbas and Silas...having written **through** their hand (Greek: *dia cheiros autōn*) Acts 15:22-23.

Here, to 'write through' meant that the Aramaic-speaking James instructed Barsabbas and Silas to express his resolutions to the Gentile churches in their language, Greek.

It is likely that Peter intends his readers in Anatolia to understand that he has entrusted Silvanus with a similar task in respect of them. If that is correct, it means Peter would have indicated the content and nature of this letter to Silvanus, and that Silvanus has expressed these in his own words. This would mean that while the letter came with the authority of Peter, the actual words came from Silvanus.

Many have wondered how an uneducated Galilean fisherman would be able to write a letter as polished as First Peter. One satisfying explanation is that Peter wrote the letter 'through' an experienced person like Silvanus, who was Greek-speaking and who had already co-authored two letters. See page 130.

Furthermore, in *ca.* 49, following the Jerusalem Council, Silvanus not only wrote the encyclical letter for James, he also delivered and explained it to these northern, Greek-speaking churches (Acts 15:23, 30-33; cf. 16:4). It is quite possible, likewise, that Silvanus, the amanuensis who wrote the letter, also carried it to these Anatolian provinces, on Peter's behalf, explaining its message to the people from church to church.

## GREETINGS FROM BABLYLON (5:13)

*5:13 She who is at Babylon, who is likewise chosen,*
*sends you greetings;*
*and so does my son Mark.*

'Babylon' is Peter's code word for Rome, the world metropolis, from which he is sending this letter to the Anatolians.

By New Testament times 'Babylon' had become a symbolic name for wicked human power that rejects God and seeks to oppress God's people. This was the 'Babel' where the unrepentant clustered together and sought to 'make a name for themselves', erecting a city with a tower to reach the heavens (Genesis 11:4; cf. 10:9-10). This was the Babylon to which captives from Jerusalem were taken in exile, where they wept (Psalm 137:1). Babylon was the place where its inhabitants shook their fists in the face of God, claiming they were forever safe from his judgments (Isaiah 47:8).

Evidently, for the early Christians 'Babylon' came to symbolise Rome since the book of Revelation also identifies

Rome in that way (Revelation 14:8; 16:19; 17:5; 18:2, 10, 21).

The 'fiery ordeal' that signifies the *beginning* of judgment (4:12,17) suggest that such sufferings had commenced in Rome. The various references to 'suffering' (insults, public abuse, magistrates' trial) that are happening in Anatolia had begun to happen in Rome. If the 'same experience of suffering that is required of your brotherhood throughout the world' (5:9) is falling on the Anatolians, we conclude it had begun to fall on believers in Rome.

Therefore, for the Anatolians to receive a letter from Babylon was tantamount to receiving a letter from hell! That, however, is comforting. If Peter, Mark, Silvanus and the Roman believers can cope (by God's strength) with their sufferings in 'Babylon', then so too can the Anatolians, in the strength of God.

Indeed, Peter assures them that even in 'Babylon' believers are secure. If the Anatolians are 'chosen...by God' (1:2) the Roman believers are 'likewise chosen'. The letter begins declaring that God has 'chosen' those who receive the letter and ends declaring that those from whom the letter comes are 'likewise chosen'. This is powerful evidence of the ultimate security of believers in an insecure world.

John Mark, like Silvanus, was a prominent Christian leader. He was a Jerusalemite, whose double names (Jewish and Roman) imply status and wealth. Both men were bilingual, fluently speaking and writing both Aramaic and Greek. Like Silvanus, John Mark had previously accompanied Paul on missionary journeys (Acts 12:25; 13:5, 13; Colossians 4:10), before his present association with Peter. John Mark was the son of Mary in whose home Peter had presided at a gathering of believers (Acts 12:12). This may be the reason Peter calls him 'my son'.

Like Silvanus, Mark was also an amanuensis for Peter. Whereas Silvanus wrote First Peter, Mark wrote the Gospel that bears his name.[35] Both the letter and the Gospel,

35. Our source for this is Papias, Bishop of Hierapolis, writing *ca.* 110 (see Eusebius, *History of the Christian Church* 3.39.12-16).

however, were written (in Rome) under the authority and direction of Peter.

## FINAL GREETINGS (5:14)

*5:14 Greet one another with the kiss of love.*
*Peace to all of you that are in Christ.*

Finally, Peter encourages them to 'greet one another with the kiss of love'. Clearly such a greeting was widespread in the early churches since Paul gives the same encouragement in Romans 16:16, 1 Corinthians 16:20, 2 Corinthians 13:12, and 1 Thessalonians 5:26.

This 'kiss' expresses their relationship with one another in the family of God. They are a loving brotherhood (1:22; 2:17; 4:8). Their love for one another is the sign that each serves the one Lord and prays to the one Father.

Last of all Peter declares God's 'peace to all who are in Christ'. On the night he was arrested Jesus told Peter and the other disciples that in him they would have peace because he had overcome the world (John 16:33). In the thirty years since then Peter had known peace of heart despite many sufferings and from his own experience he pronounces his benediction of peace upon those who are 'in Christ'.

Peter's prayer for their 'peace' and Paul's for 'grace' that occur at the ends of their letters likely reflects similar liturgical endings to meetings in the various mission churches of that era.

*Reflection on verses 12-14:* Many readers switch off when they come to these final parts of letters. Yet these short passages frequently yield very important information.

Here we learn Peter's purpose in writing was 'to appeal to' his readers. Do we the modern day readers feel encouraged and challenged by Peter's 'appeal' to us to 'stand fast' in the grace of God? It is a challenge to us when we consider how costly it was to be a disciple then compared with how relatively easy it is to be one today.

We also hear from Peter his place of writing ('Babylon' =

Rome) and that Silvanus and Mark are with him, as well as other believers. We should not doubt, therefore, that First Peter is a genuine letter and that Peter is the writer (through Silvanus). Some New Testament scholars doubt this to be a genuine letter, asserting that a well-intentioned writer has written 'as if' it is by Peter, planting details about Silvanus and Mark to make it more convincing. This really is a strange idea. Peter's Anatolian readers are engaged in a life and death struggle. Imagine how they would feel if they learnt that Peter was not really the author, but that someone was cruelly pretending to be, and that he had set out to deceive them! The moral credibility of the letter would sink like a stone.

Peter's appeal to 'stand fast', his commendation of Silvanus and his relayed greetings from Mark combine to support the sense of authenticity of this letter.

# 6

# Issues in First Peter

## DID PETER WRITE THIS LETTER?

First Peter has long been recognised as impressive writing. Its Greek is of a high standard and it has many quotations from the Greek Old Testament (called the Septuagint, abbreviated as the LXX). Its author is an accomplished writer of the Greek language and a biblical scholar.

Its supposed author Peter was the fisherman from Galilee. The religious leaders of Jerusalem scorned him as 'uneducated' (Acts 4:13). Could that man write this letter?

We must not underestimate Peter. His home was Bethsaida, a town where many people spoke Greek. His original name Simon and his brother's name, Andrew, were commonplace in Greek circles. Peter may have been uneducated, but that does not mean unintelligent; many great scholars had humble origins. The scornful remark that he was 'uneducated' really means he was not a graduate of the rabbinic academies of Jerusalem.

As well, Peter became the daily companion and disciple of the greatest rabbi of all, Jesus of Nazareth. Who can estimate the effects on Peter of the intellectual and spiritual exposure to Christ that he sustained over a three to four year period?

When we add to this Peter's years of experience as the leading apostle in the land of Israel for the first decade and a half, followed by his extensive travels afterwards, we can begin to accept the possibility that Peter could have written this letter entirely on his own.

But did Peter, in fact, write the letter?

Through careful research some scholars are questioning

whether Peter's Greek is quite as sophisticated and 'pure' as previously thought. (See Karen J. Jobes, 'The Syntax of 1 Peter: Just How Good is the Greek?' *Bulletin of Biblical Research* 13/2 (2003), 159-173.) Through that research it appears that the Greek of First Peter has a decidedly Semitic tone and that it falls behind the excellent Greek, for example of the Letter to the Hebrews. The same research coincidentally equated the standard of First Peter with First Thessalonians, finding about the same quantity of Semitic constructions as in that letter.

That research has tended to lower our view of the purity and excellence of the Greek of First Peter. In turn, this makes direct authorship by Peter more imaginable. Despite this, however, the standard of Greek in the letter remains relatively high and, in my opinion, presents a stumbling block to direct Petrine authorship.

On balance I remain persuaded by the 'Silvanus' hypothesis, usually associated with Edward Gordon Selwyn's commentary published in 1961. As noted in my comments on 1 Peter 5:12, Silvanus was a Jew who spoke Aramaic and Greek and who co-authored First and Second Thessalonians and who had been entrusted to write and deliver the encyclical from the Jerusalem Council to the Greek-speaking churches of Syria and Cilicia. This person could have written First Peter.

Peter's high regard for Silvanus and his disclosure that he had written to them *through* him is best interpreted along these lines.

I see a parallel between Peter and the Jewish historian Josephus, who like Peter came to Rome, though about a decade after the writing of First Peter. Like Peter, Josephus' first language was Aramaic. Most likely both men knew enough Greek to speak and perhaps read, but not enough to write in Greek. When Josephus moved to Rome (in his late thirties) he set out to learn Greek grammar, followed by the study of Greek prose and poetry. In his book *Antiquities of the Jews* he confesses that habitual use of his mother tongue prevented him gaining precision in pronunciation.

Nonetheless, when Josephus came to write *Jewish War* in the mid-70s he wrote in the Aramaic language. That edition has not survived. Subsequently, Josephus re-wrote the *Jewish War* in Greek, though with the help of those he calls 'co-workers', 'for the sake of the Greek' (*Against Apion* 1.50). So superior is the Greek syntax in the *Jewish War* that it is difficult to believe Josephus could have been the primary writer. The credit for that must be given to his unnamed 'co-workers'.

My contention is that something similar happened with Peter. Most likely Peter's grasp of Greek improved over the decade or more as he moved away from Palestine into Greek-speaking Syria, Anatolia (?) and Greece. Even in Rome, where Latin was the native language, it is clear that Greek was widely spoken there as well.

Like Josephus Peter had 'co-workers', though he does not describe them in those terms. Accomplished as writers in Greek, Silvanus and Mark interpreted and set out Peter's teaching, as a letter and as a Gospel. The Letter was written and sent while Peter was still alive and, as a result, bears his name and therefore his authority.

Peter's involvement in the writing of the Gospel of Mark was less direct. Most likely Peter had arranged for Mark to write his Gospel after Peter's death based, however, on the apostle's preaching. In his Second Letter Peter wrote, 'I know that the putting off of my body will be soon...I will see to it that after my departure you may be able at any time to recall these things' (1:14-15). Irenaeus, an early authority who had also visited Rome, understood Peter's words to refer to the Gospel of Mark. In *Against Heresies* Irenaeus wrote, 'after the *death* of Peter...Mark, the disciple and interpreter of Peter transmitted to us in writing the things preached by Peter'. Tertullian, another early authority wrote in *Against Marcion* that Mark's Gospel could be called Peter's Gospel.

In short, Peter's last years in Rome were associated with literate and scholarly colleagues like Silvanus and Mark who interpreted and transmitted the teaching of the old apostle into the First Letter of Peter, on one hand, and the Gospel of

Mark, on the other. The former was published during Peter's lifetime, the latter posthumously.

Would Silvanus' collaboration with Peter affect our view of First Peter as canonical Scripture? I see no problem here since the text was sent under the authority of Peter the apostle of the Lord.

## FIRST PETER IN THE EARLY CHURCH

Two statements can be made confidently about the attitude of post-apostolic Christians to First Peter: (i) Peter was regarded as its author, and (ii) the letter was as widely quoted and referred to as any book in the New Testament, the Gospels included.

1. The earliest evidence for the existence and authorship of First Peter is found in Peter's reference in Second Peter to 'this second letter' (2 Peter 3:1).

2. Polycarp, Bishop of Smyrna, writing early in the second century, quotes many times from First Peter (Polycarp, Philippians 1:3; 2:1-2; 6:3; 7:2; 8:1-2; 10:2-3).

3. Papias, Bishop of Hierapolis, also writing early in the second century refers to Peter's first epistle (referred to in Eusebius, *History of the Christian Church* 2.15.2).

4. Later in the second century there are extensive references to Peter's letter in the voluminous writings of Irenaeus (*Against Heresies* 4.9.2; 5.7.2) and Tertullian (*Scorpiace* 12).

We could go on, but the point is made. There is considerable evidence in support of this letter's existence and authorship by Peter. From the beginning of its life, therefore, First Peter was received and affirmed as a genuine letter by Peter.

## A SCRIBAL SCHOOL IN ROME?

Peter wrote to the Anatolian provinces 'through Silvanus' sometime in the mid-60s, that is, about thirty years after the historical life span of Jesus of Nazareth.

Study of this letter has yielded two apparent contradictions. On one hand much of the letter (about 40 percent) echoes Jesus' teachings and the letters of Paul (in particular, Romans, Ephesians and 1 Thessalonians) and the letter of James. Those echoes, however, prove not to be from the *text* of the Gospels or the letters of Paul or the letter of James, but rather from earlier and independent traditions that must have been circulating by the 40s (since Paul and James also echo them). To put it another way, Peter is echoing traditions that the Gospels and the letters of Paul and James also echo.

On the other hand Peter's writing style is uniform throughout. This appears to be a contradiction since we assume that a large amount of 'echoed' material would dislocate Peter's text. But First Peter is seamlessly consistent from beginning to end. This means that Peter has absorbed almost half the contents of his letter from outside sources, yet in such a way that we could not identify these extraneous elements unless we had observed the points of contact in Peter's text in those other texts.

From this we make two observations.

First, the author of First Peter was a gifted writer, who has managed to create a unified and polished piece of work. For that is what it is. For me, First Peter is a glittering diamond in the jewel box of the New Testament.

Second, Peter (and his associates Silvanus and Mark) had access to many early traditions that he skilfully adapted in his letter for the pastoral needs of his Anatolian readers.

In addition to these many pre-existing Christian traditions that Peter incorporates he quotes various Old Testament texts (1:16/Leviticus 11:44; 1:24-25a/Isaiah 40:6-8); 3:10-12/Psalm 34:12-16; 4:18/Proverbs 11:31). Furthermore, Peter creates an elaborate teaching about Christ the 'stone' (2:4-8) by citing and connecting Isaiah 28:16; Psalm 118:22 and Isaiah 8:14. To these (in 2:9-10) he adds citations from Isaiah 43:20-21; Exodus 19:6; Hosea 1:9; 2:1). Peter often uses briefer Old Testament texts, notably in 2:21-25 where he echoes words and phrases from Isaiah 53 and from Deuteronomy 21:23. Clearly, too, the Flood narrative (Genesis 6-8) informed Peter's typology in 3:18-22. Almost all Peter's Old Testament citations and allusions are from the Greek version of the Old Testament (called the Septuagint or LXX).

My strong impression is that Peter and his colleagues in Rome were accomplished and diligent scholars of both the Greek Old Testament and the many written apostolic traditions that were then in circulation (and that would soon also become fixed in the writings of James, Paul and the Gospels, as we now have them).

The text of First Peter dispels the myth that the early Christians were uneducated yokels. The unified style of First Peter, the many Old Testament quotations and various apostolic traditions point to a scribal community that would have been similar to the scribal schools of the Pharisees in Jerusalem and the monastic school of the Essenes at Qumran near the Dead Sea. Whereas the scholarship of the Pharisees' and the Essenes' was dedicated to a wide spectrum of Old Testament texts, the scholarship reflected in First Peter was even more comprehensive. Its other chief distinctive was that it arose from love for Jesus and a passion to support and strengthen his people in times of persecution.

# 7

# Themes in First Peter

## CHRIST AND TIME

It is important to understand Peter's idea of time. According to Peter there is an immeasurable expanse of time *before history began* and immeasurable expanse of time *after history ends*. God is the master of history, the expanse of time in which we live, but equally he is master of the aeons before and after history. He determines when history begins, when it ends and what happens within history.

Central in God's purposes before and during history is Jesus Christ, the Son of God (1:3), the elect and precious One (2:4).

> [Christ] was destined before the foundation of the world
> but was made manifest at the end of times for your sake (1:20).
> Christ suffered for sins once and for all (3:18).

God had predetermined Jesus' appearance within history and his suffering for sins 'once and for all' before the creation of the universe.

Prior to Jesus' appearance, at an earlier stage within history, the prophets were moved by the Spirit of Christ to work out when Christ would come and how he would suffer and be glorified by resurrection and ascension (1:10-11).

Christ is likewise central at the end of history. Though at present veiled from sight by his resurrection and ascension there is a coming 'day of visitation' (2:12) when the 'chief shepherd will be manifested' (5:4). Christ will be 'revealed at the last time' (1:5, 7) bringing the 'grace' of 'salvation' to those who belong to him (1:9, 10, 13).

Peter has a majestic view of Christ as the one chosen by

God in the aeons before history so as to enter history as the suffering Saviour, who as glorified at this present time will bring history to its appointed end, and with that 'end' (4:7), the salvation of God to those who during their lives had 'come' to Christ, the living stone (2:4).

## LIVING HOPE FOR FOREIGNERS AND EXILES

Peter addresses his readers as 'aliens and exiles' (2:11) who are living throughout the 'time of exile' (1:17) as a group 'scattered' or 'dispersed' (1:1) amongst the 'Gentiles' (2:11; 4:3).

The two keywords 'aliens and exiles' mean the same thing and refer to foreigners living in another country where they are not citizens and have no rights.

Some scholars have attempted to find a literal meaning in these words. In *A Home for the Homeless: A Sociological Exegesis of 1 Peter, its Situation and Strategy* J.H. Elliott has proposed that 'aliens and exiles' were poor rural folk in Anatolia, who recently had been disenfranchised. Apart from being based on conjecture, this theory fails to explain the implied wealth of the women who must put aside valuable jewellery (3:1-6). More elaborately, in her commentary on 1 Peter, K. Jobes suggests (i) that the recipients were converted ex-Romans forced or encouraged by Emperor Claudius to colonise the Anatolian provinces, and (ii) that some had belonged to Peter's sphere of influence in Rome. While plausible, there is no evidence in support of Jobes' reconstruction.

These and other theories relating to 'aliens and exiles' fail to account for the metaphorical use of similar terminology in other parts of the Bible. For example, Paul addresses his readers as former 'strangers and foreigners' (Ephesians 2:19). Both Peter and Paul are likening believers to the patriarch Abraham who came to live in Canaan, but was a foreigner there (Genesis 15:3; 23:4; cf. Psalm 39:12; Exodus 2:22).

We conclude that Peter means his readers then and now to understand that they are 'foreigners' in this present world, in whichever nation that might be. God has promised them a 'land' which is 'imperishable, undefiled and unfading' and which cannot be taken from them (1:4-5), but which is not yet theirs. It is a 'salvation ready to be revealed at the last time' (1:5). God has re-birthed them for this hope through the gospel-word, based on the resurrection of Christ from the dead (1:3).

Accordingly, they are to turn their backs on 'passions of the flesh that make war on the soul' (2:11), 'passions' that were the hallmark of their 'former' lives (1:14, 18) and are the current preoccupations of their contemporaries (4:3). This does not mean hostility toward society at large. On the contrary, these 'foreigners' are to live as model citizens who are respectful of current expressions of government (2:13-17).

It is possible that Peter has in mind Jeremiah's words to the 'exiles' from Jerusalem in faraway Babylon, that they were to 'seek the welfare of the city and pray to the Lord on its behalf' although this was not their true homeland (Jeremiah 29:7).

## ISRAEL'S 'STORY' REPEATED

Peter reveals a deep knowledge of God's dealings with his people Israel. This should come as no surprise since Peter was an Israelite, a member of that nation. What does surprise us, though, is the degree to which Peter sees the 'story' of Israel being spiritually repeated in the experience of Christian believers. They are God's new 'nation' and 'people' (2:9).

(i) Peter knew that just as God 'chose' Israel (Deuteronomy 7:7), so too he had chosen the new Israel. He begins his letter addressing 'the chosen ones' in the Anatolian provinces and he concludes by sending a greeting from those likewise 'chosen' in Babylon (Rome). Previously God dealt with an identifiable nation, which was composed of one race, whereas now this 'people' is composed of Jews and Gentiles and is 'scattered' among the nations. Nonetheless, God still chooses those who are to be his people.

(ii) As a boy attending synagogue school Peter would have marvelled at the story about Noah who built the ark to save his family from the waters of the great flood. Peter said that the water of the flood through which Noah's family were saved points onwards to the water of baptism through which believers are saved (3:20-21). Of course, the baptismal water has no saving power in itself, but rather pointed to the 'washed' conscience of the believer. Peter's way of making this point seems unusual to us, but was a 'typology' familiar to Jews at that time.

(iii) Peter also knew of Abraham's journey from Ur of the Chaldees to Canaan, the land God promised him. Although living there Abraham remained a 'sojourner' who did not even own land for the burial of his wife Sarah (Genesis 23:4; Psalm 105:12). Peter likens his readers to Abraham, as landless aliens and exiles who did not enjoy the citizenship rights of the peoples among whom they lived.

> Peter, an apostle of Jesus Christ, to the *exiles of the Dispersion* (1:1).
> ...conduct yourselves with fear throughout *the time of your exile* (1:17).
> ...I beseech you as *aliens and exiles* to
> ...maintain good conduct among the Gentiles (2:11-12).

Peter calls these 'aliens and exiles' a 'brotherhood throughout the world' (5:9; cf. 2:17).

(iv) Peter reveals his sense of the importance of Israel's 'redemption' by this reminder to the believers in Anatolia:

> You know that you were ransomed from the futile ways inherited from your fathers...with the precious blood of Christ...a lamb without blemish or spot (1:18-19).

Just as God ransomed his people long ago from slavery in Egypt (by the blood of the Passover Lamb) so now he demonstrates that same character as rescuer by liberating believers from 'futile ways' (by the blood of Christ, the spotless 'lamb').

(v) Peter continues to pick up that Old Testament 'story' by alluding to the covenant God made with the people at Mt Sinai, a covenant he sealed with the blood of oxen sprinkled on the people and on the book of the covenant (Exodus 24:1-8). At that time God declared himself to be 'holy' and that his people were to lead holy lives (Leviticus 19:2). According to Peter, God has again 'sprinkled...blood', though now it is the blood of Christ that is metaphorically 'sprinkled' upon believers who are dedicated to God in holiness by the Holy Spirit:

> ...chosen and destined by God the Father
> and sanctified by the Spirit
> for obedience to Jesus Christ
> and for sprinkling with his blood...(1:2).

> ...but as he who called you is holy,
> be holy yourselves in all your conduct;
> since it is written,
> 'You shall be holy, for I am holy' (1:15-16).

God is, as he was, the God who establishes a covenant with his people, based on his holiness, which they are to express 'in all [their] conduct'.

(vi) The Hebrews' 'exodus' from Egypt led them via Mt Sinai eventually to Canaan, the 'Promised Land'. Sadly, however, the people soon broke their covenant with God by worshipping the fertility gods of the Canaanites. In consequence they corrupted and defiled the beautiful and good land God had promised them. Peter teaches that God has renewed his 'promise' of a land to his people which, however, will not be defiled or corrupted, and which will not be taken away from them because it is being 'kept' for them in heaven:

> Blessed be the God and Father of our Lord Jesus Christ!
> By his great mercy we have been born anew to a living hope
> through the resurrection of Jesus Christ from the dead,
> and to an inheritance which is imperishable, undefiled, and unfading, kept in heaven for you...(1:3-4)

The resurrected Jesus is God's pledge of this pristine 'inheritance', the 'salvation ready to be revealed in the last time' (1:5). God gives this 'living hope' to those he 're-births', which he does through his gospel message (1:23, 25; also 1:12).

(vii) Peter continues his rehearsal of Israel's history by pointing to the temple and the priests' offering of sacrifices there, though with radical changes under the new dispensation:

(a) The company of believers is the 'house' of God; previously the temple was an actual building.
(b) The community of believers is the priesthood; previously priestly functions were limited to an individual tribe, the descendants of Aaron.
(c) The sacrifices are the gathered congregation's praise to God for his 'wonderful deeds' by which he 'called' his people out of the futility of their former lives into his wonderful light:

> ...be...built into a spiritual house
> to be a holy priesthood,
> to offer spiritual sacrifices acceptable to God
> through Jesus Christ (2:5).
>
> ...you are...a royal priesthood...
> that you may declare the wonderful deeds of him
> who called you out of darkness into his marvellous light (2:9).

Under the new dispensation the temple becomes the people, the priesthood becomes the people and the sacrifices become words of praise from grateful lips.

In conclusion, note the non-sequential nature of Peter's allusions to the 'story' of the Old Testament people. Peter does not pick up elements in that 'story' in the order in which they occurred (as I have done in the survey above). Nonetheless, Peter is deeply aware of that 'story' which he so pointedly repeats throughout his letter, but with radical adjustments appropriate to the new dispensation. Despite those adjustments we recognise God's consistency of character. God continues to choose, redeem and liberate a people, from whom he expects holiness in every aspect of their lives.

## WINNING OTHERS

(i) Peter addresses his readers as 'newborn babies' (2:2) who owe their spiritual 're-birth' to the Gospel message that had been proclaimed to them (1:25; 1:12).

As a consequence the 'passions of...former ignorance', those 'futile ways passed on from their fathers' belong to their pre-baptismal past (1:14, 18). Peter urges them not to return to those bad old days when they lived in drunkenness, carousing and lawless idolatry (4:3-4).

(ii) Many people have heard the same message who 'do not believe', having 'disobeyed the word' (2:7-8). In their rebellion they continue in their alcoholic and sexual excesses, along with their worship of pagan gods (4:3-4). These disbelievers in turn 'blaspheme' their former drinking and womanising associates (4:4; 2:12, 15; 3:16), most likely pricked in conscience by the repentance of these 're-born' ones. Some appear to have gone so far as to complain to the authorities about the believers' 'strange' behaviour with the result that legal action had been taken against them, necessitating their formal 'defence' (3:15).

(iii) It is clear from First Peter that these Christians in Anatolia were facing local persecution. At the same time, Peter (in company with other apostles) expected believers to 'win' unbelievers to the faith. That is an onerous task at the best of times, but it was especially challenging when believers were at a disadvantage, as they were when Peter wrote this letter.

Peter is following a convention of the time in addressing believers in terms of their various social relationships, whether as citizens to the provincial authorities, as slaves to owners or as wives to husbands. Those conventions were set out by moralistic writers of those times in what have come to be called 'house tables'. Only in the most superficial sense, however, are we to think of Peter's words as a 'house table'.

In Peter's hands we see that in each relationship the believer is at a definite disadvantage (except husbands, 3:7). At that time the power of the governor over locals was absolute (except in the rare circumstance where one happened to be a

Roman citizen) and where the power of the *Paterfamilias* was absolute in regard to his wife, his children and his slaves. Those having authority were not required to be accountable regarding their treatment of those 'beneath' them.

(iv) Peter teaches two closely connected patterns of behaviour to 'win' others, in particular those who held the whip hand in these various relationships. Peter exhorted the citizen to 'be subject' to the governor, the slave to the owner and the wife to the husband (2:1-17; 18-25; 3:1-6). This is more onerous than an admonition to be 'obedient' since that could be merely passive 'eye service' (Ephesians 6:6). To 'be subject to' was comprehensive but it implied a degree of willingness as well as an element of discretion whereby one could refuse to comply with a demand to commit a crime or participate in an immoral or heretical act (for example, 4:15-16).

Peter's encouragement to 'be subject', which Paul also uses in his letters, doubtless sprang from Jesus' words to 'render to Caesar' the payment of taxes (Mark 12:16-17) and Jesus' example in 'submitting' to the God-given authority of Pontius Pilate (John 19:11).

Second, the apostle calls for citizens, slaves and wives experiencing oppressive behaviour from those in power over them to follow Christ's model when facing death. Peter urges citizens to give a fearless confession with 'gentleness' (3:15), recalling Christ's own 'gentleness' (Matthew 11:29). To women married to unbelievers, including those who inspire terror (3:6), Peter exhorts them to have a 'gentle...spirit' (3:4), where once more Christ's own 'gentleness' is in mind. Peter gives the most detailed encouragement to the slave suffering unjustly from a harsh owner (2:18). He is to look to Christ's behaviour at Golgotha as a template to copy, a living example to follow closely (2:21). For though he was scorned in his suffering, Christ neither returned abuse nor threats, but with quiet dignity and faith handed his just cause over to God (2:22-23).

In other words, Peter is directing citizens, wives and slaves to imitate Christ so as to replicate his 'patient' behaviour in his dire circumstances at Golgotha.

(v) Peter's encouragement that wives 'win' their unbelieving husbands (assumed also by Paul in 1 Corinthians 7:16) points to an expected mission intent from citizens to 'win' persecuting authorities, from wives to 'win' harsh husbands and from slaves to 'win' cruel masters. Each is to seek to 'win' their oppressors to Christ.

It would not usually have been possible to 'preach' Christ in those circumstances, but the very harshness and injustice citizens, slaves and wives suffer provides the opportunity to *live* Christ towards oppressors, so as to preach Christ 'wordlessly' (3:1).

Peter knows well that only the Gospel-word, when welcomed, brings re-birth (1:12, 25). Yet he is also conscious of the huge impact of Christ-like behaviour on both believers and unbelievers. Many an unbeliever will see the 'good deeds' of the believer and become a re-born Christian and so glorify God on the 'day of visitation' (2:12).

## HOLINESS IN ALL LIVING

In the story of the old covenant God called upon his 'now-redeemed' people at Mt Sinai to 'be holy' because he is 'holy' (Leviticus 11:44-45; 19:2; 20:26; 21:8). In parallel to this Peter calls upon the 'now-obedient' children (of God) 'be holy yourselves in all your conduct' (1:15). Significantly Peter's call for holiness sets the tone for all that follows. This was anticipated at the head of the letter. God chose them to be 'sanctified [set apart] by the Spirit' (1:2) for holiness. They are a 'redeemed' and 'purified' people (1:18, 22) for ways of life that are truly 'different' from what they had been previously and that are different from the lives of those among whom they live as sojourners.

1:13 Therefore...1:14 as obedient children,
do not be conformed to the passions of your former ignorance,
1:15 but as he who called you is holy, *be holy yourselves in all your conduct*;
1:16 since it is written,
'You shall be holy, for I am holy.'

So God is calling his chosen ones to a life of holiness. What does Peter mean by this?

This call is based on their re-birth by the preached Gospel-word (1:12, 23-25; cf. 2:4, 8; 3:1; 4:17), which was accompanied by the 'reply of a good conscience' at their baptism (3:21). These people had come to know in their 'consciences' of God's forgiveness of the past sins; they were re-born people.

Peter's admonition 'be holy' implies a reversal of the practices of their 'former lives'. Pre-baptism their lives were marked by 'ignorance [of God (1:14)]', 'passions' (1:14; 2:11; 4:2), their 'inherited empty way of living' (1:18) and their sexual licentiousness, drunkenness and idolatry (4:2-4). Peter's injunction 'be holy' implies their determination to know God and to master their 'passions' as they turn decisively from the emptiness and futility of the conduct of parents and friends.

This will also be expressed in the way they live in the community of believers. They are to display 'fervent, unhypocritical love' towards the 'brotherhood' (1:22; 2:17) as they reject malice, deceit, hypocrisy, envy and slander (2:1) but rather engage with them in 'unity' with 'sympathy, love, compassion and humility' (3:8). They are to pray for their brothers and sisters showing 'forgiving love', 'hospitality', 'serving of one another' in teaching and practical help (4:7-11). They will be humbly submissive to the leadership of their presbyters (5:1-5).

Equally, holiness in 'all their conduct' will find expression in their behaviour in society, hostile though it is towards Christians. They will be 'subject' to the Emperor and his surrogate governors. In the same vein, the slave will be subject to his master and the wife to her husband even in situations where the master and the husband respectively are harsh in their behaviour. Peter explicitly teaches against any form of vengeance by Christian citizens towards local leaders, slaves towards masters or wives towards husbands. Rather, they are to trust God's ultimate justice as they humble themselves under his mighty hand.

There is a robust even non-religious character to this

'holiness'. In brief, it is the very behaviour and demeanour of Jesus himself. His is to be the example of 'holiness' that they will follow in 'all their conduct'.

## GOD ACCORDING TO FIRST PETER

Peter's letter is saturated with references to God, so much so that it is difficult to know where to start to summarise his teachings.

These teachings are precisely what we would expect from one who:

(a) was a Jew steeped in the Old Testament
(b) was a disciple of the Lord Jesus
(c) had become an experienced church leader and pastor tempered in the fires of suffering.

We should keep in mind, however, that many of Peter's readers were Gentiles who had previously been idolaters and for whom the biblical view of God was quite new.

(i) It is likely significant that Peter's earliest references to God are in Trinitarian terms (though he does not use the word 'trinity'). This is consistent with other New Testament writers who are convinced that God has engaged with humanity 'down here' in the coming of his Son into the world and the activity of the Spirit of God within human hearts.

While the Godhead is a unity, the Father exercises primacy in choosing believers to be 'sanctified by the Spirit' for 'obedience to Jesus Christ' (1:2). The Spirit works in the heart to bring about obedience to Jesus Christ and so fulfil the holy purposes of the Father for his chosen ones.

Since God is the Father of Jesus Christ, it follows that he is his Son (1:3). The Spirit is the source of sanctification and therefore holiness (1:2, 15-16). As well, having inspired the prophets to identify the coming Christ in his sufferings and glory (1:11), the Spirit enables preachers to proclaim him (1:12). The Spirit of God rests on those faithful believers who are reviled for the name of Christ (4:14).

(ii) God 'destined' his Son to be 'manifested' in history 'before the foundation of the world', 'ransomed' those in slavery by his death and raised him alive to give them living hope (1:18-21). Having proclaimed his victory to 'spirits in prison' Christ is at God's right hand, with angels, authorities and powers subject to him (3:22).

(iii) God is also Father to those children he mercifully re-births through the living word of the Gospel (1:25; cf. 1:3), as proclaimed by human messengers (1:12). These are now obedient children who have left behind the emptiness and futility of their former wicked lives (1:14, 18; 4:3-4). God guards his children for the pure inheritance he has marked out for them (1:4)

To those he re-births God gives 'living hope' beyond the grave (1:3), as well as a new family of believers (1:22; 4:7-11) which is a brotherhood throughout the world (2:17; 5:9; 4:7-11).

(iv) Just as the LORD who redeemed his people from Egypt was 'holy' and expected 'holiness' from his people, so too is the One now revealed as the 'God and Father' of the Lord Jesus Christ. Although he is their 'Father' they must not forget to 'fear' him since he is the 'Holy One' who judges each one impartially (1:16; 2:17). His now regenerated children must not return to their bad old ways, but be obedient to him in all their conduct.

(v) Mindful of his mercy towards them, God's rescued people as priests offer 'spiritual sacrifice' of praise to God for his mighty acts of salvation (2:5, 9-10).

(vi) Those who suffer unjustly like Christ are to conduct themselves under their sufferings as he did, so as to point others to him by that example. As God's 'servants' and 'mindful' of him, they do his 'will' in all things (2:15-16). In particular, they glorify God as they suffer as Christians, blameless in all things (4:16), walking in humility 'under h[illegible] mighty hand' (5:6).

(vii) In the 'end' God the just judge will punish the wicked (4:5) and will vindicate his unjustly suffering Son (2:23) and his unjustly suffering children (4:19).

(viii) In God's sight a 'gentle and quiet spirit' like Christ's is 'precious' (3:4). God's eyes are upon the righteous and his ears are open to their prayers (3:12). He cares for his children in their sufferings (5:7).

(ix) Let God's children find assurance that God is 'all powerful' but also 'the God of all grace' who will 'strengthen' them through their ordeal and finally 'exalt' them (5:6, 10-11)